CHRISTIAN FAMILY ACTIVITIES

for families with preschoolers

by Wayne Rickerson

STANDARD PUBLISHING
Cincinnati, Ohio
2963

Library of Congress Cataloging in Publication Data

Rickerson, Wayne
    Christian Family Activities for families with preschoolers.

    1. Family—Religious life. I. Title.
BV4526.2.R53   249   82-5583
ISBN: 0-87239-568-5   AACR2

CONTENTS

Building a Positive Relationship With Others 53

THE NIGHT CHILDREN LOVE BEST

Our youngest daughter, Bridget, a spunky little four-year-old, had fallen and skinned her already bruised elbows and knees. The pain this time was a little more than she could bear.

"Daddy," she cried, "I want it to be Family Night."

"Why do you want it to be Family Night?" I questioned.

"Because Family Night will help my arm feel better," explained Bridget.

Now, I'm not claiming that your children will ask for a Family Night to cure their hurts, but I will promise this: Your young children will love Family Nights!

Bridget, now ten years old, is just as enthusiastic about Family Night as she was when she was four. In fact, we are now starting our eighth year of regular Family Nights. I can honestly say they have been a great contribution to our family life. Our children are now ten, fourteen, and fifteen, and we are still going strong.

Over the past eight years I have helped thousands of families start Family Nights. Parents of families who have committed themselves to Family Nights and followed the guidelines have enjoyed great success. Comments are usually, "We just can't believe how our children love Family Nights!"

Recently the Mills Family started Family Nights. After playing the game "Spin the Bottle" (included in this book), Tara threw her arms around her dad in her exuberance over Family Night and said, "Daddy, I love you!"

What makes Family Nights, these once-a-week family times, so popular with children? *First of all, and most important, Family Nights are fun.* I'd like to repeat this so you never forget it. Fun, fun, fun,

fun! Let's face it. Young children learn largely through play. Family Nights include play. An important goal is for your family to have fun together.

Second, the family is sharing in an activity together. This is very important to children. Ask any group of children, "What makes a happy family?" The most common answer will be "Doing things together."

A third factor that contributes to the popularity of Family Nights is that *the children are active participants, not just spectators.* It is their night! They get to express themselves by doing such things as discussing, playing games, drawing pictures, acting out Bible stories, singing, serving dessert, and displaying a special talent.

Fourth, I believe Family Nights are popular with children because *God blesses these times together.* Most Family Nights are based on God's Word, and God is clear about what His Word will do. "My word . . . shall not return to Me empty, without accomplishing what I desire, and without succeeding in the matter for which I sent it" (Isaiah 55:11).

God wants us to share His Word with our children and if we are diligent in doing that He will succeed through us.

Janet and I have seen many benefits from our Family Nights. We have all learned God's Word together. Family Nights have been a tool to increase our skills in discussion and communication. Our children have learned how to lead as they have taken responsibilities for Family Nights. Creativity has blossomed as each family member has been encouraged to express himself in various ways. Self-esteem has been nourished as each family member has been made to feel important. And through all this the family has been brought closer together.

Four Keys to Successful Family Nights

Commitment
Unless you commit yourself to a weekly Family Night, I guarantee you will not be successful. Schedules will interfere. You will be amazed how many times your Family Nights will be interrupted.

If you commit yourself, however, to a weekly Family Night, then nothing will interfere. This is what commitment is all about.

Perhaps you are a young couple with lots of family time right now. You might be asking, "What's the big deal about one night a week? We're together almost every night." I can remember those days, but they won't last! Someday you will be fighting for family time. Then you will be glad you established the tradition of Family Night when your children were young.

Fun

Above all, have fun. You are centering Family Nights around the needs of your preschool children. Preschoolers learn through play. It is easy for us to get so intent on "teaching a lesson" that we forget to have fun. Our own worst Family Nights have occurred when I have tried to get too "heavy." If you plan to have fun and keep things simple, the learning will follow.

Participation

Preschoolers do learn through second-hand experiences—seeing and hearing. But, they learn far more through first-hand experiences—doing. That young child of yours wants to *do* something. Pack your Family Nights with action. Let your children do as much as possible. Besides the suggestions given in each Family Night plan, find ways your young child can participate. Allow your child to pray, serve dessert, sing a song, do a talent show, tell a joke, or color a picture.

Flexibility

Be flexible. Try various approaches. Learn what works best with your own children. Perhaps you have more than one young child. You will have to gear the material and activities to meet at least some of the needs of each child. Flexibility will help you find what works best for your family.

How to Use Family Night Plans

There are fifty-two Family Night plans in this manual. Each Family Night has a topic based on one of the eight loves I will share in chapter two. These eight loves will assist you in helping your child reach the "three great life goals" I will describe in the next chapter. You may use them in any order you wish. Browse through the plans and start with the ones you feel your children will enjoy most. Do complete one unit before going on to another. This will be less confusing to your child.

In order to make God's Word important to your young child, always have a Bible at hand as you tell Bible stories. Use a Bible he can handle, and one you can highlight the "Bible words" in. Then help your little one to "read" the highlighted words. He will enjoy this and will soon learn the words. Use the Bible words and the important thoughts from the Family Night throughout the week. The lesson will be reinforced every day.

Feel free to use any part of a Family Night. Some of the activities, for example, will be too advanced for a very young child. Note the frequent suggestions to be used with toddlers, those who are twelve months to twenty-four or twenty-six months old. Learn to adapt the material to the age of your child or children.

One more thought. Do a lot of things outside during the summer. We have found great success over the years by going to a summer Family Night schedule, which means going places—parks, boating, hiking, miniature golf, picnics, swimming, and so forth.

Let me say a word at this point to those of you who have babies. Don't wait until later to start Family Nights. Start now! You and your spouse sit down with that precious baby and have a Family Night the

© 1980 VOLK

first week of his life. Here are some suggestions of what to do. Sing a song about Jesus to your baby. Talk to your baby about God. Tell him that God made him. Remember that from the very first day of his life he is learning the building blocks of language. He can also learn the building blocks of God.

As your baby gets a little older, show him pictures of Jesus (mounted on cardboard and covered with clear adhesive-backed plastic) and talk about God's special book. Your baby will sense your love for God, for Jesus, and for the Bible.

Spend a few minutes with your spouse talking about your goals for your baby. Have prayer together for yourself as parents, and for your child.

Right now this Family Night might take just fifteen minutes, but as your baby grows, the time you spend together on Family Night will also grow. In an incredibly short time your baby will be a toddler, a school-age child, a teenager, a young adult. Take advantage of every opportunity God gives you to teach Christian values and build family unity.

HELP YOUR CHILDREN REACH THREE GREAT LIFE GOALS

You feel the urgency to teach Christian values to your children. You are motivated to start Family Nights. You want God's best in your young children's lives. You want your children to be committed to Christ. "But, how can we do this?" you ask yourself. "What concepts can my child really learn about God? What goals should I set?"

These are the questions Janet and I have asked ourselves. Probably most of you have asked yourselves some of the same questions. Even though we may be committed to teaching Christian values to our children, it is difficult to know where to start. In this chapter I will attempt to answer these questions by sharing with you "Three Great Life Goals," and eight building-block concepts that can help you reach these goals. You will see how Family Nights can be effective teaching tools.

Throughout your child's life you will be teaching him three basic relationships—his relationship with God, his relationship with himself, and his relationship with others. Jesus talked about the importance of all three of these relationships when He was asked, "Which is the great commandment of the Law?"

Jesus answered, " 'You shall love the Lord your God with all your heart, and with all your soul, and with all your mind.' This is the great and foremost commandment. And a second is like it, 'You shall love your neighbor as yourself.' On these two commandments depend the whole Law and the Prophets'' (Matthew 22:37-40).

Jesus is saying that there are three truly vital areas in our lives: our love for God, our love for others, and our love for ourselves (implied). The development of these relationships is your child's life goal. How well your child learns these relationships will determine the quality of his Christian life and his success as an individual.

Three Great Life Goals

A Personal Relationship With God

Goal one is the goal of all goals. This is the foundation of the other two goals. Without a personal relationship with God through Jesus Christ, your child will never be at peace with himself or with his fellowmen.

A Positive Relationship With Self

A crucial element in your child's development is what he thinks about himself. This is called self-esteem, or his self-image. One of the greatest gifts you can give your child is to help him develop a positive view of himself. If he feels good about who he is, if he can "get along" with himself, then the next goal is much easier to reach.

A Personal Relationship With Others

We spend our entire lives relating to others. For those who have never learned to develop personal relationships with others, life is full of pain. One of the greatest joys of life is the ability to become intimate with other persons. Yet many people go through life without the ability. Throughout your child's life you will be teaching him these "three great life goals." To show how you, as a parent, fit into this process, I have developed the "Pyramid of Life Relationships" shown.

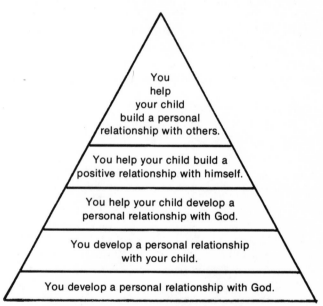

Pyramid of Life Relationships

The bottom line of the pyramid is that you develop your own personal relationship with God. This is essential for teaching your children the three great life goals. We cannot pass on what we do not have. But when we have a vital relationship with Christ, we can share that relationship with our children. Their first glimpse of God is in us. The best way we can help our children develop a personal relationship with God is for them to see God as an active, vital part of our own lives.

Second, you develop a personal relationship with your child. God comes to us and offers us a personal relationship with Him. Then, because of that relationship, He teaches us a Christian life-style through His Word. We must use the same model when teaching Christian values to our children. At level two, develop a warm, loving, giving relationship with your children—a human model of God's love for us. Then based upon that relationship, our children will be wide open to our helping them develop a personal relationship with God. Without that loving relationship with your child, any teaching you try to do simply will not work. The relationship always comes first!

The fact that I can work effectively with Heidi, Liesl, and Bridget is a result of the tremendous amount of time I invested in them when they were very young. We played hide and seek, went on hikes, made forts, had special times, went out to breakfast, and did a host of other things together. These were all ways to build a personal relationship with each child. Because of the relationship, they are open to what I want to teach them about Christ.

Third, help your child develop a personal relationship with God. Based upon your personal relationship with God and your personal relationship with your child, you teach your child how to develop a personal relationship with God. You share God through the example of your own life. You talk about God to your child. You read Bible stories to your child. You eventually lead your child to Christ and then help him grow toward Christian maturity.

Fourth, help your child develop a positive relationship with himself. You are the greatest influence on how your child feels about himself. You are the most important person in his life. You can help your child develop a good self-image if you have a growing personal relationship with God, if you are developing a warm personal relationship with your child, and if you are helping your child develop a personal relationship with God. God makes your child feel special. You make your child feel special. God accepts your child unconditionally. You accept him unconditionally. These are great foundations for a healthy sense of self-esteem.

Fifth, you help your child build a personal relationship with others. The four previous levels have prepared your child for level five. He should be growing in his ability to get along with others. Now, at times I'm sure you may wonder about the job you've done, especially if you are the parents of a two- or three-year-old. Don't panic. Two is a dis-

ease, and your child will soon grow out of it! Each year you will see your child grow in his ability to build positive relationships with others.

Three Methods to Reach the Goals

In Scripture God has given us three methods by which these goals, and all Christian values, can be taught.

Model
"Hear, O Israel! The Lord is our God, the Lord is one! And you shall love the Lord your God with all your heart and with all your soul and with all your might. And these words, which I am commanding you today, shall be on your heart; and you shall teach them diligently to your sons and shall talk of them when you sit in your house and when you walk by the way and when you lie down and when you rise up. And you shall bind them as a sign on your hand and they shall be as frontals on your forehead. And you shall write them on the doorposts of your house and on your gates" (Deuteronomy 6:4-9).

Notice that parents were to "love the Lord" first and to have God's Word written on their hearts. The next step was to teach these things to their children. Here we find the first principle of teaching Christian values to our children: *Teaching by example or model.*

We are to model God's love and His words to our children. That means our lives have to be in line with what we say we believe. No amount of great Family Nights or other types of teaching will ever overcome our actions not matching our words. Modeling vital Christian faith is our greatest way to teach Christian values to our children.

Teach
A second method of teaching is given in Deuteronomy 7:6, 7. Parents were to "teach them diligently" unto their children. This suggests a structured teaching situation, a time set aside by parents to share God's Word with their children. Family Nights and other types of family Bible reading/discussion are ways to "teach diligently."

Talk
A third method is found in verse 7. God's people were to "talk" of God's words to their children. They were to talk of them while they were sitting, lying down, walking, and getting up. In other words, they were to teach informally in all of life. Teaching Christian values to our children is much

more than a Family Night or Family Devotion. It is more than our example. It is also the discussion and application of God's Word to our lives. All three methods are important. I like to visualize the three methods as fitting together in a teaching life-style as shown.

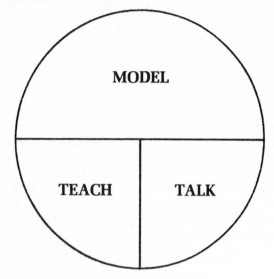

Building-Block Concepts —The Eight Loves

We have discussed the three great life goals that you are to help your child achieve. We have just mentioned the three primary teaching methods that are taught in God's Word. Now I want to share eight building-block concepts that are the subject matter or curriculum to help us reach the three goals. These building-block concepts I call "The Eight Loves." Your children can start learning these early in life and then build on them as they continue to mature. The Eight Loves are:

1. A love of God
2. A love of Jesus
3. A love of God's world
4. A love of God's Word
5. A love of prayer
6. A love of self
7. A love of family
8. A love of others

First, your child must develop a love of God. He needs to see God as a loving heavenly Father who loves and cares for him personally.

Second, your child needs to develop a love for Jesus. When he is very small he will love the "baby Jesus." As he grows he will learn to love Jesus as God's Son who died on the cross for his sins.

Third, your child needs to develop a love of God's world. He needs to learn to see God's handiwork in nature. He needs to see that God provided us with this beautiful world because He loves us. Because of this we must take care of God's world.

Fourth, your child must develop a love of God's Word. He needs to see it as a special book. In this special book God tells us that He loves us, and gives us instructions on how to live.

Fifth, your child needs to develop a love of prayer. He needs to understand that he can communicate with God and that God listens and will answer his prayers.

Sixth, your child needs to develop a love of himself. This means he must see himself as a special person, uniquely created by God—so special that Jesus died for him.

Seventh, your child needs to develop a love for his family. He needs to see that God created the family and that family members need to live in harmony, loving one another.

Eighth, your child needs to develop a love of others. He must see that the true mark of a Christian is the love he shows for his fellowmen. By loving others he shows his love for God.

Putting It All Together

Each of the eight loves can be taught by the three methods given in Deuteronomy 6:4-9. Take, for example, love number six, A Love of Self. First, I must *model* this in my own life. If my child does not see me accepting myself, how can I ever teach him to accept himself? If he cannot accept himself, how will he learn to love the God who made him? For that matter, if I do not accept myself then I will probably have a difficult time accepting my child.

I can use the second teaching method, *teach* (a formal teaching). I could have a Family Night on self-image. A Family Night on self image is included in this book.

I can also *talk* about how special my child is. This would be using the third method of teaching Christian values. For example, as I put my child to bed I might say, "Amy, you are very special. I love you just the way you are." Or, as Susan is coloring a picture I might say, "Susie, what a nice picture. No one else could color that just like you are doing. You are very special."

If you had done the above you would have used all three methods of the teaching life-style. Each method has its place in teaching Christian values.

I like to picture the process of helping your child achieve the three great life goals in the following way:

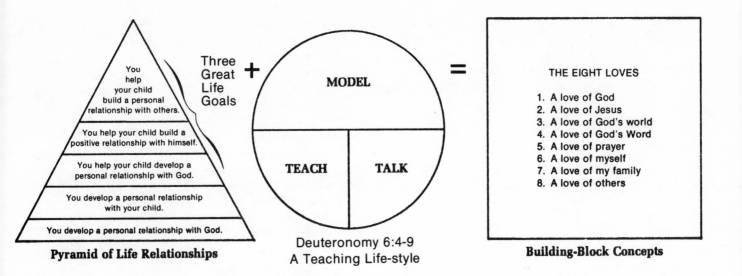

Pyramid of Life Relationships

Deuteronomy 6:4-9
A Teaching Life-style

Building-Block Concepts

I sincerely believe that, if you will commit yourself to working with God to help your child attain these three great life goals, your children will become committed Christians.

God's Word will not return to Him empty without achieving what He desires. And certainly, God desires that our children love Him, love themselves, and love others.

BUILDING
A PERSONAL RELATIONSHIP
WITH GOD

GOD KNOWS EVERYTHING

GOAL
To help your family understand that God is all-knowing

BIBLE WORDS
"God . . . knows all things" (1 John 3:20).

Memorize this together by saying it aloud several times. If you have a beginning reader in your family, put the words on small cards and let him arrange them in correct order. Glue pieces of magnetic strips to the backs of the cards and keep them on the refrigerator as a reminder for your child during the week.

FAMILY ACTIVITIES

I Know!

Start your Family Night by asking the following questions. When a child knows the answer he says, "I know!" and answers.
1. Where was Jesus born? (Bethlehem)
2. On what special day do we celebrate Jesus' birth? (Christmas day)
3. What was the name of the boy who played the harp and took care of the sheep? (David)
4. Who made the animals? (God)
5. What does your daddy do?
6. What does your mommy do?
7. How many people are in your family?
8. What color is water?
9. What color is the sun?
10. Who is Jesus' Father? (God)

What Do Mommy and Daddy Know?

Each child gets to ask Mommy and Daddy one difficult question.

When you have completed these activities, discuss the fact that there are many things we do not know, but that God knows everything.

What God Knows

God knows all about us. He even knows how many hairs are on our heads. (Let your children try to count the hairs on your head just to see how impossible it is. For those of you men with whom it is a possibility, my apologies!)
1. God knows our names.
2. God knows what we think.
3. God knew about us before we were born.
4. God knows how long we are going to live.
5. God knows how the world was created.
6. God knows how many stars there are.

Let your children add to the list. Just marvel together at a God who is all-knowing.

If your preschoolers are very young, try to have several storybooks with suitable pictures of people and animals, and other of God's creations. For example, *God's World, God's Animals,* and *God Loves Us* have pictures that can be used to talk to your little ones about what God knows. "God knows how to make trees. . . . God knows all about doggies. . . . God knows Mommy's name. . . . God knew about Mark (use child's name) before he was born!"

Learn to adapt this material to fit the needs of younger children. Particularly remember to keep your Family Night activities as short as possible to fit the attention span of your preschooler. Use much repetition tonight and throughout the week to help your child or children remember the concept you have introduced.

Because God Knows

Share with your children the confidence that we have because God knows everything.

Teach your family the little song, "God Cares." Then thank God that He not only knows all about us but also cares about us.

God Cares

UNIT 1: A Love of God

GOD WANTS US TO GO TO CHURCH

GOAL
To help family members realize it is important to go to church

BIBLE WORDS
"Let us go to the house of the Lord" (Psalm 122:1).

FAMILY ACTIVITIES

Play Church

Tell your children that you are going to play church. Help them to think about what they do at church. Remember, your preschool child will have a totally different schedule of activities from yours. Let him, with some prompting, tell what happens in his classroom. This will probably include a play time (learning centers), worship time with songs, prayer, and a couple of action rhymes, the Bible story, a craft, and so forth.

Sit in a circle on the floor and talk about what he does in his classroom. Sing a song and do an action rhyme he has learned at church (ask his teacher ahead of time, if necessary), and help him "read" from his Bible the Bible words for tonight.

Then explain that you will have church like the big people do. Have the children help you arrange your room for a church service. Let an older child be the preacher, let someone lead a song or two, someone else pray, and so forth. Tell the preschool child just what is going on. This can be a good introduction to grown-up worship if he is not used to being in adult church.

After you have had your church service, ask each person to tell what he likes best about church. Your preschooler may need some help with this.

My Church

Roll out a long piece of paper on the floor. Mark off a two-foot section for each family member. Explain that everyone is to draw a picture of a church building and put inside it his favorite things or people.

For a younger child, draw an outline of a church building. Give him magazine or catalog pictures of people to glue in his church building.

When the project is complete, tape the mural to a wall. Have each one tell about his church.

Have everyone repeat the Bible words. Discuss why it is important to go to church.

If your little one is restless, play a singing game to the tune of "Mulberry Bush." "This is the way we go to church, go to church, go to church, etc., so early Sunday morning." You can pretend to walk, with Bibles under arms, or drive to church (the mural). Let your children make up verses.

Church Action Rhyme

Teach this action rhyme to your family:

Here Is the Church

Here is the church,
  (Hands together, fingers interlocked inside.)
Nice as can be.
  (Put up two forefingers for steeple.)
Open the door,
  (Open hands.)
And you will see me.
  (Hold up forefingers.)
                              —Sylvia Tester

Prayer

Have each person pray, thanking God for "our special church."

15

MAKE-A-HAPPY-SOUND NIGHT

GOAL

To help your children realize that we make God happy when we make "happy sounds" for Him

BIBLE WORDS

"Sing for joy to God" (Psalm 81:1).

FAMILY ACTIVITIES

Start your Family Night by talking about the many kinds of "happy sounds" we can make for God. Say that a long time ago people made happy sounds to God by singing, shouting, and playing instruments. Read Psalm 81:1-3.

King Hezekiah's Happy Day

For the benefit of your preschool child or children, tell this abbreviated story of King Hezekiah and the worship that followed the restoration of the temple in Jerusalem (2 Chronicles 29:28-30). Remember to hold the Bible in your hands as you tell the story.

King Hezekiah and his friends went to the temple together. They went to worship God. It was a happy day!

The singers sang a happy song. The trumpeters played a happy song. King Hezekiah and all the people were very happy. They were happy because they could sing and worship God, just the way God had said to do.

Ask your children some questions about what King Hezekiah and his friends did to make "happy sounds" to God.

Family Rhythm Band

Tell your children you are going to make "happy sounds" to God by having a family rhythm band. Put some pots and pans face down on the floor and give one of the children a wooden spoon to beat on the pans. Another child might like to use two lids for cymbals. Two teaspoons make good rhythm instruments, as do a set of metal measuring spoons. Look around the house for other instruments for your band.

Songs

Tell the children that a happy sound God likes to hear is our singing to Him. Sing some of the children's favorite songs, such as "Jesus Loves Me," "Praise Him, Praise Him," and "Jesus Loves the Little Children of the World." Your preschooler may prefer to use the rhythm instruments to singing. He probably will not do both at one time.

You might want to buy a special children's record to listen to tonight. Preview the record before playing it for the family.

Make a Megaphone

Let your children make a megaphone to help them sing "happy songs" to God. Use paper cups with handles. Cut out the bottoms of the cups ahead of time. Let the children add decorative seals. Then repeat a favorite song using the megaphones.

GOD SAVES NOAH AND THE ANIMALS

GOAL

To help the family to know God loved and cared for Noah and to lead them to feel thankful for His love and care

BIBLE WORDS

"He cares for you" (1 Peter 5:7).

FAMILY ACTIVITIES

Tell this story about Noah to begin your activities. If you have very young children, omit the part about the people being so wicked, and dwell only upon God's care of Noah. Your little ones will probably not question why Noah and his family were in the ark. If you prefer, make the ark to use as a visual for the story. Or, read one of the books mentioned at the end of this page.

God Cares for Noah

Can you imagine a world in which almost everyone did nothing but bad things? Well, that's how people acted in Noah's time. God became very angry and decided to send a flood that would destroy the world.

There was one man and his family who pleased God. That man was Noah. God told Noah to make a big ark-boat. He told Noah to make room in the ark-boat for his family and for two of each of the animals. Noah did what God told him to do.

When Noah and his family and all the animals were inside the ark-boat, it began to rain. It rained for many days and nights. Even the trees and mountains were covered with water. Then the rain stopped. The ark-boat floated on the water. Noah and his family and the animals were safe inside the ark-boat. God was taking care of them.

Finally the water began to go down. The ark-boat came to rest on a mountaintop. Noah sent out a dove to see if the water was low enough for him to leave the ark-boat. When the dove did not come back, Noah knew the dove must have found a tree. So Noah and his family and all the animals got out of the ark-boat to make new homes.

Noah prayed, "Thank You, God, for taking care of us in the ark-boat. Thank You for loving us."

Build an Ark

Get a large cardboard box. On one side draw a large opening. Cut across the top and down both sides and then score across the bottom to make a ramp for the animals. Cut one window in the box.

On pages 71 and 73 you will find pairs of animals. Cut these out and hide them throughout the house. Tell your family that they are to find two animals of the same kind and put them in the ark-boat.

When you have found all the animals and put them in the ark-boat, put Noah inside. Ask your children what it would have been like on the huge boat. How would Noah have felt? A little bit afraid? Let them tell about times they feel afraid. What would it have sounded like on the ark-boat? Have each person make the sound his favorite animal makes—all at once!

Let one of the children pretend to fly a dove out the window and find a "tree" to land on. Then each family member can take the animals out to make new homes. Have Noah say a thank-you prayer.

Make a Rainbow

Give your family members paper and crayons or magic markers. Let them draw rainbows. You may have to draw this for young children and let them scribble-color. Tell how God put a rainbow in the sky as a sign of His promise never to cover the earth with another flood.

Prayer

Have everyone thank God for His love and care for Noah and for them.

Storybooks About Noah

The Big Flood and *The Great Big Boat* are simple enough for preschoolers. *Ark Full of Animals* is a favorite of young children because of the flaps that can be opened to reveal surprises.

GROWLING STOMACHS

GOAL
To help the family know that God supplies our needs

BIBLE WORDS
"God shall supply all your needs" (Philippians 4:19).

FAMILY ACTIVITIES
You will have to prepare ahead of time for this Family Night. You will be using the story of the children of Israel in the wilderness to teach that God always supplies our needs—specifically food. Post an "Off Limits" sign in your kitchen or whatever room you plan to use. Place vanilla wafers or some type of dry cereal around the room to represent manna. Also set out pieces of beef jerky or lunch meat to represent the quail.

Growling Stomachs
Tell the following story to the children:

Has your stomach ever growled? How does it sound? *(Have everyone make a growling sound.)* Our stomachs usually growl when we are hungry.

A long time ago God's people had growling stomachs. They were traveling in the wilderness where it was hot and dry. Their food was all gone. They were very hungry. Their stomachs hurt because they were so hungry.

The people grumbled to Moses, "We are hungry! We had more food than this when we were slaves!"

God heard the people and He told Moses, "I will rain bread from Heaven for the people to eat." Can you imagine bread "raining" from the sky? God also gave them meat every day.

Shhh!! Listen. *(Have everyone be very quiet.)* There are no more growling stomachs! God gave food to His people until they reached the promised land.

Manna March
Explain to the family that you are going to search for manna and meat in the wilderness. First, go into several rooms where there is no food. Then go into the room where you placed the food.

Let the children gather the "manna and meat." Sing to the "Mulberry Bush" tune: "This is the way we pick up our food, etc., so early in the morning."
As everyone eats, discuss the story:
—Why were the people hungry?
—How did God give them food?
—Why doesn't God give us food from Heaven?
—How does God give us food?

How God Gives Us
Read one of the books from the "How God Gives Us" series, such as *How God Gives Us Apples.*

Prayer
Have a circle of prayer with each person thanking God for supplying our needs, or giving us food.

I Thank God

S. T.   SYLVIA TESTER

I thank God. I thank God. I thank God.

WE CAN TRUST GOD

GOAL
To help your children realize that they can always trust God

BIBLE WORDS
"Trust in the Lord" (Psalm 37:3).

FAMILY ACTIVITIES

Secret Adventure Night

Select a secret adventure for your children. If it is summertime, a park with a swimming pool, the mountains, a stream or a lake would be good. Pack a picnic lunch. Tell your children that you are going on a secret trip. Promise them they will have fun. They will try to guess where you are going. Just tell them that they must trust you.

If the weather does not permit you to take an outdoor excursion, plan to drive to a "secret" destination, perhaps the church building. Or, simply blindfold your children and lead them about through the house, perhaps ending up in the basement. Keep reminding them that they must trust you.

For outdoor fun, take a large rubber ball to play with your preschooler. Throwing bean bags into a cardboard box is fun outdoors or indoors.

The Candy Tree

While you are having fun playing outdoors, have your spouse or another adult slip away from the group and find a tree with low branches or a bush. Place some small pieces of wrapped candy on the branches. Then have that person call the children and tell them about this "candy" tree or bush. The children will have a great time picking the candy, trying to guess where it came from.

Indoors, simply hide candy or some other treat about the "secret" destination or in another room. Let the children have a hunt.

The Story of Abraham

Have your family sit down and tell them the story of Abraham from Genesis 12:1-5.

God spoke to Abraham and told him to move to a new land. Abraham did not know where the new land was or how long it would take to get there. He didn't even know the way to the new land. God promised to show him the way and take care of him. Abraham trusted God.

Abraham and his wife, Sarah, packed everything they owned—their tents, their clothing, their pots and pans, their food—everything! Then Abraham and Sarah and all their servants began the long trip. The sheep and cattle and goats went too.

Abraham and Sarah traveled a long way. They trusted God and God took care of them. Many good things happened because they trusted God.

If you have a photo album of vacation pictures, look through this and talk about how different our travel is from Abraham's. Ask the children if they think Abraham drove a car. Were there restaurants along the way? motels?

Now remind your children that they trusted their father (or mother) today and some good things happened. They can trust their heavenly Father, God, too. Their heavenly Father always does what He says He will do.

A Quiet Time

Some time during the day or evening, when your children need a quiet activity, read the book *What Is Faith?* It will help your young child understand the meaning of trust.

Action!

Teach your family this simple action song. Use it after you have been sitting a while.

Family Fun

J. B.   JEAN BAXENDALE

Mom-my can jump, And I can too. Dad-dy can run, And I can too.
We jump and jump, And run and run. Our fam-i-ly has lots of fun!
Jump, jump, jump, jump, jump, jump, jump, jump! Sit down!
Run, run, run, run, run, run, run, run!

19

GOD WANTS US TO BE HAPPY

GOAL

To remind family members that happiness is a choice God wants us to make

BIBLE WORDS

"Blessed [happy] is he who trusts in the Lord" (Proverbs 16:20).

FAMILY ACTIVITIES

Give each child a paper plate. Show him how to draw a happy face on one side and a sad one on the other side. If your children are young, make pencil outlines for them to follow with crayon.

Happy and Sad Stories

Tell your children some stories about happy and sad children. They are to decide whether the child in the story is being happy or sad. When a child decides, he should hold up the face that is like the child in the story.

Story #1: Bobby's mother asked him to pick up the toys in his room. Bobby yelled, "I'm too tired!" and stomped away.

Story #2: When Amy got out of bed in the morning she said, "It's a beautiful day! I'm going to be kind to everyone today."

Story #3: Billy fell down and skinned his knee. It hurt and he cried. Then Billy said, "My knee still hurts a little but I'm going to try to be happy anyway."

Story #4: Heather had to go to the store with her mother. This made Heather angry because she wanted to play. Heather fussed all the time.

Discuss:

—How could Bobby be happy?
—How could Heather be happy?
—When we feel unhappy, how can we feel happy again?

Happy Practice

Tell your children that you are going to hold "Happy Practice." When you turn the paper-plate sad face toward them, they are to act sad. When you turn the happy face toward them, they are to act happy. After you have done this several times, discuss with your children the fact that we don't have to stay sad. We can change and be happy if we want to.

Things That Make Me Happy

Tell your family that one way to become happy when we are sad is to think about happy things. Let each family member tell about things that make him happy.

More Happy Activities

Let your children choose a game to play that makes them happy. See the list of children's games on page 68.

Learn the song "I'm So Happy Today." If your toddler is too young to sing, encourage him to clap his hands as you sing, or provide him with a rhythm instrument, perhaps a bell.

Read the Happy Day book, *What Is Love?*

I'm So Happy Today

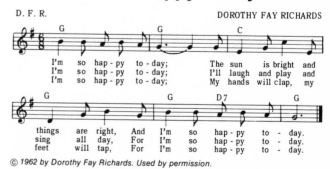

D. F. R.   DOROTHY FAY RICHARDS

I'm so hap-py to-day; The sun is bright and
I'm so hap-py to-day; I'll laugh and play and
I'm so hap-py to-day; My hands will clap, my

things are right, And I'm so hap-py to-day.
sing all day, For I'm so hap-py to-day.
feet will tap, For I'm so hap-py to-day.

© 1962 by Dorothy Fay Richards. Used by permission.

HAPPY BIRTHDAY, JESUS

GOAL
To help family members experience the joy of celebrating the birth of Jesus

BIBLE WORDS
"He [God] loved us and sent His Son" (1 John 4:10).

FAMILY ACTIVITIES
Tell the following account of the birth of Jesus, or read it from the Bible (Luke 2:1-20).

Joseph and Mary had traveled a long way. Step, step, step, step they went. They were so tired! When they came to Bethlehem, they wanted a place to stay, but the town was full of people!

Joseph wanted a comfortable place for Mary to stay because she was going to have a baby. The only place Joseph could find was a stable where the animals were kept.

Joseph spread a blanket on the hay to make a bed for Mary. While they were there, Jesus was born. Mary put Him to bed in a manger filled with hay.

There were shepherds nearby taking care of their sheep. An angel came to them. The shepherds were afraid! The angel said, "Do not be afraid. I have good news for you. Today a baby has been born in Bethlehem. He is a very special baby. He is your Savior, Christ the Lord."

The shepherds hurried to Bethlehem to see this special baby. They found Him lying in a manger, just as the angel had told them. The shepherds were happy. They thanked God for the baby Jesus. Then they went out and told others about Him.

Jesus' Birthday Play
Have a family play about the birth of Jesus.

Scene #1: Mary and Joseph travel to Bethlehem. Since we don't know whether or not Mary rode on a donkey, just have the actors walk.

Scene #2: Joseph looks for a place to stay. The innkeeper can kindly offer his stable. Joseph prepares a bed for Mary.

Scene #3: The baby Jesus is born. Use a box filled with hay or a substitute, such as raffia. Use a baby doll for Jesus. Mary and Joseph are very happy. Maybe Mary can sing a lullaby to baby Jesus.

Scene #4: The angel appears to the shepherds. They are afraid. Have the angel make his speech, with a bit of prompting. Have the lights turned off and let the angel hold a flashlight to set the stage.

Scene #5: The shepherds hurry to see baby Jesus. They say thank-you to God for Jesus.

Scene #6: (optional) Let the shepherds go out and tell others about Jesus. This would be good practice for your little ones to express to someone that Jesus is born.

Nativity Scene
If you do not have one, purchase a nativity scene from a Christian bookstore. Let your children move the figures as they retell the story of Jesus' birth.

Birthday Party for Jesus
Help your children decorate for Jesus' birthday party. Use balloons and crepe paper just as you would for a family birthday celebration. Bake a birthday cake ahead of time. Put one candle on the cake. Let a child light the candle. Sing "Happy Birthday" to Jesus. Thank God for sending Jesus.

Let your children give a gift to Jesus. Many churches collect food, clothing, and toys to give to the needy at Christmastime. Explain to your family that for Jesus' birthday Jesus wants us to give His presents to those who are poor. If you use this material at another time of year, send the money to a Christian home for children if you have no local work to give to.

Giant Birthday Card
If you have time, make a giant birthday card for Jesus. Use a large sheet of newsprint or butcher paper. Fold it like a card. Let your children draw pictures for Jesus on the card. Maybe they could even make up a little verse for their card.

Christmas Storybooks
Baby Jesus was written especially for young preschoolers. *Baby Jesus ABC Storybook, The Very Special Night, The Gift of Christmas,* and *Christmas Is a Time for Singing* are all suitable for 3s and up.

GROWING AS JESUS GREW

GOAL

To help your children understand that Jesus was a real person who did not stay a baby but grew as they are growing

BIBLE WORDS

"Jesus grew in wisdom and stature, and in favor with God and men" (Luke 2:52, NIV).

FAMILY ACTIVITIES

Preschool children usually have difficulty in connecting the baby Jesus with the man Jesus. They seem to feel that these are two separate people. The story of the boy Jesus helps tie Jesus' life together. This story (based on Luke 2:40, 52) also will help your children think about Jesus as a real child, who grew in the same ways they are growing.

The Boy Jesus

Have several pictures of one or all your children at different ages. Ask them if they stayed babies or are growing up? After they assure you they are growing up, remind them that Jesus was a real person who did not stay a baby either.

The Bible tells us that Jesus grew bigger and stronger every day, just as you are growing. Jesus learned many things too.

Jesus probably helped His mother around the house. What do you suppose He did? Jesus probably helped Joseph in his carpentry shop. Joseph made furniture and tools of wood. Perhaps Jesus carried wood for Joseph. Mary and Joseph were pleased with Jesus. He obeyed Mary and Joseph.

As Jesus had more birthdays, He grew bigger and bigger. He learned more ways to help and to be kind. The Bible says that everyone liked Jesus, and most important of all, God was pleased with Him.

Discuss:

—How did Jesus grow?
—What did Jesus learn to do? (Mention normal activities such as walking, talking, helping, etc.)
—Did people like Him?
—Was God pleased with His Son?
—How are you growing?

Grow Chart

Cut a length of paper longer than your tallest child. Print at the top, "(Names) are growing as Jesus grew." Fasten the paper to a wall. Have each child stand in front of the chart to be measured. Put his name beside his height. Measure the children again in a few months to show how they have grown. Let the children decorate the grow chart with crayons, colorful seals, or pictures cut from magazines or old take-home papers.

Carpenter's Helpers

Get out the building blocks and pretend to be carpenters and helpers. Tell the children that Joseph was a carpenter and that Jesus helped him in his shop. Show the children how to pretend to saw and hammer, or use toy tools if your children have these.

Look Who's Growing!

Take time to look at the children's photo albums tonight. Show them how they are growing and changing. Remind them they are "big enough" to do things for themselves, to help others, and so forth. Being big enough to do certain things is important to a preschooler. Make these positive statements rather than "You're big enough to stop sucking your thumb." Talk about the many things your children have learned since they were babies.

If you have an album of your own pictures, your children would enjoy seeing how Dad or Mom grew up.

Read a Story

Growing as Jesus Grew and Growing Up will both fit with tonight's theme. If you don't have either of these, try to find a book that shows Jesus as a baby, as a boy, and as a man. Jesus, God's Son, a surprise book, is a good example of this.

Dessert

Encourage the children to help serve and clean up after the dessert because they are "big enough" to be helpers just as Jesus was.

FOLLOWING IN JESUS' STEPS

GOAL

To help family members see that they must follow Jesus' example

BIBLE WORDS

"Follow in His steps" (1 Peter 2:21).

FAMILY ACTIVITIES

Follow the Leader

Let each family member have a turn being the leader. The leader should do something that everyone can copy (scratch his head, jump, crawl, and so forth). The rest of the family must do what the leader does.

Simon Says

This is another good game to illustrate the concept of following a leader. This will be difficult for a very small preschooler.

We Must Follow Jesus

Explain that it is fun to play "Follow the Leader" and "Simon Says," but our real leader is Jesus and we must follow Him.

Tell about the time Jesus walked by the Sea of Galilee and called two brothers, Peter and Andrew, to come and follow Him. They left their nets and followed Jesus (Matthew 4:18-22).

Jesus is not here on earth in a body that we can see, so we can't follow Him that way. But we can follow Him by doing what He wants us to do. How do we know what He wants us to do? Yes, the Bible tells us.

Jesus' Footprints

Cut out life-size paper feet (see sketch). On each foot write one of the following:

Be kind.
Be helpful.
Love one another.
Obey your parents.

Explain to your children that each footprint tells us something Jesus wants us to do. Read the first message and let a child put it on the floor. He then must jump from that footprint as far as he can. Then the second child or family member puts the next footprint where the first child landed. Repeat this procedure until all the footprints are on the floor.

Have your family suggest ways they can be kind, helpful, loving, and obedient.

Prayer

Have the family pray together, with each person asking God to help him follow in the footsteps of Jesus.

Sing the song found on page 29 using the words "Follow Me" instead of "Come to Me."

Application Stories

To your older preschoolers and beginning readers, read *Buzzy Bee Storybook,* and *Buzzy Bee Says "Bee Happy."* These stories give everyday examples of following Jesus.

JESUS KEEPS HIS PROMISES

GOAL
To help family members realize that Jesus always does what He says He will do

BIBLE WORDS
"He who promised is faithful" (Hebrews 10:23).

FAMILY ACTIVITIES
It is important for you to remember that a preschool child does not understand promises as an adult does. Perhaps you have noticed that a promise to your child is a temporary thing. That is the way his mind works, and it simply has to be accepted. Some day he will understand the full significance of a promise.

Even though they don't understand this concept, we must try to teach young preschoolers about promises. This will be the foundation of their thinking as they mature. For tonight's session, explain that a promise means that if you say you are going to do something, you do it.

A Story About a Promise
Tell this story about Jesus and His friends who were fishing (Luke 5:1-11).

A crowd had gathered by the lake to hear Jesus teach. There were so many people that they could not see Jesus. Jesus got into a boat and sat down where the people could see and hear Him. After He was done, Jesus told His friends, "Take your boat out on the lake and let down your nets. I promise you will catch many fish."

Peter, one of Jesus' friends, said, "We have fished all night and caught nothing. But if You promise we will catch fish, I believe You."

So the men took the boat out on the lake and put down their nets. And just as Jesus had promised, they caught so many fish that they had to have more fishermen help them. Jesus keeps His promises!

Let's Go Fishing
Make a boat outline on the floor using wooden blocks or just a piece of yarn or string. Sit in the boat and pretend to row. Provide a "fishing pole" for one child at a time to go fishing. Put a magnet on the end of the line. Have fish cut from construction paper with paper clips on their noses. On each fish write a promise. For example:

> Jesus always loves you.
> You will be with Jesus in Heaven.
> Jesus will take care of us.
> Jesus hears us when we pray.
> Jesus will always be your friend.

You may need to guide your child's line to connect with a fish. After the children have all had turns fishing for Jesus' promises, let them fish for some treats. You might have numbers on some fish that correspond to numbers on wrapped packages of candy, cookies, a balloon, a small toy, or whatever kind of treat you want to have. Or, you can just attach paper clips to the gifts and place them in the "water" around the boat.

End your time together thanking God for Jesus and for Jesus' promises.

Colorful Fish
For your budding artists, draw large fish outlines for them to color. See who can make the most colorful fish. Or, if you prefer, have small scraps of paper to be glued on the fish. Metallic scraps make a fine fish! Tell the children they are making fish like the ones Jesus promised His friends they would catch.

JESUS HEALED THE SICK

GOAL
To help the family understand that Jesus could make sick people well because He is God's Son

BIBLE WORDS
"Jesus is . . . the Son of God" (John 20:31).

FAMILY ACTIVITIES
Start your Family Night by telling the following story from John 5:1-9.

A long time ago in the city of Jerusalem there was a pool of water called the pool of Bethesda. The people thought that a sick person could be made well by getting into this pool at a certain time.

There was a man who could not get into the pool because he could not walk. Other people always got there before he could. He had been unable to walk for thirty-eight years.

One day, Jesus came to the pool. He saw the man who couldn't walk. "Do you want to be made well?" Jesus asked the man.

"Yes," the man answered, "but I have no one to help me into the water."

Jesus said to the man, "Get up, pick up your bedroll, and walk."

The man did what Jesus told him. How happy he was! Jesus could make him well because Jesus is the Son of God.

Lame-Man Puppets

Make a "lame man" for each of your children. You will need a piece of construction paper, chenille wires, tape, glue, and crayons.

From the construction paper cut two triangles, according to the diagram. Cut holes for fingers as shown. Tape the chenille wire to the back of one triangle as shown, then glue the two triangles together with the chenille wire inside. Cut a circle 2 inches in diameter and draw features on it. Then glue to the triangle. Make one of these to represent Jesus too.

If you prefer, use a piece of cloth in place of one of the paper triangles so the figure will have a textured feel that preschoolers love. You could even add yarn hair and beards.

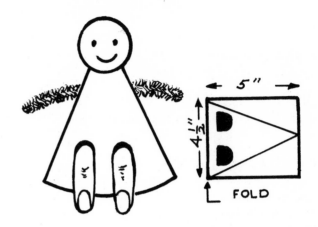

Let your children act out the story using the puppets. Have a flat pan of water for the pool, and a cloth bedroll.

Sing a Song

To the familiar "Mulberry Bush" tune sing these words: "Jesus made the lame man walk, lame man walk, lame man walk, etc., because He is God's Son."

Prayer

Have each person thank God for His Son, Jesus, who could make the lame man walk and sick people get well.

UNIT 2: A Love of Jesus

WHEN YOU ARE AFRAID

GOAL
To help your children know that Jesus can help them feel unafraid

BIBLE WORDS
"I am with you always" (Matthew 28:20).

FAMILY ACTIVITIES

Guess My Fear

Tell each person to think of something he is afraid of, but not to say it out loud. Start with one child and have each family member guess what his fear is. Each person can have two guesses. If no one guesses, then the person must tell the fear he was thinking of. Don't let anyone make fun of another's fears.

Jesus' Friends Were Afraid

Tell the story of Jesus' stilling the storm (Mark 4:35-41), or read the story in a Bible storybook, such as *Jesus, God's Son,* or from the Scriptures (a modern translation).

Next, explain that you are all going to pretend that you are Jesus' friends. Have a large cardboard carton to be the boat. Have everyone get in the boat, if possible, and then turn off the lights. Rock the boat and make storm sounds (but don't scare a young preschooler). After a minute or two say, "Don't be afraid, I am with you. Storm, be still!" Then turn on the lights.

Discuss:

—How did you feel during the storm?
—How did you feel when you heard the voice and the lights came on?
—How do you think Jesus' friends felt during the storm?
—How did they feel after they saw Him make the storm quit? (Tell what the Scripture says about this.)

Talk about how Jesus is always with us, even though we can't see Him. We can ask Jesus to help us when we are afraid. He can help us feel quiet inside.

Rock the Boat

If you have very young children, let them play with small boats in a pan of water. Talk about how Jesus made the storm quit. Say, "He can do that because He is God's Son."

Books

Now would be a good time to read several books about being afraid and about having courage. Two good books to use are *When I'm Afraid* and *Courage.* Sometimes, being able to talk about a particular fear is the first step in overcoming it. Learning to go to God and Jesus in prayer and trusting them are both important concepts for young children to learn.

Close with a time of prayer, asking Jesus to help you not feel afraid about things.

Jesus Is God's Son

BARBARA EBERT
Arr. by MORINE BARNES

26

THE LOST SHEEP

GOAL

To remind your family of the great love God and Jesus have for them

BIBLE WORDS

"He first loved us" (1 John 4:19).

FAMILY ACTIVITIES

Cut out the sheep found on page 69 and hide it in your house.

Tell your family that there is a poor little lost sheep somewhere in the house. Everyone must look for it. If someone gets close to the sheep, you will go "Baaaa."

When the sheep has been found, tell the story of the lost sheep from Luke 15:4-6. If possible, use a children's storybook, such as *The Little Lost Lamb,* to tell the story. Put the emphasis on the love the shepherd had for his sheep, and not on the rejoicing in Heaven when a sinner repents. Preschoolers will not understand this.

Explain to your children that Jesus and God love us just as the shepherd loved his sheep. Preschoolers will not need or be interested in a lengthy explanation or sermonizing.

Spool Sheep

Let your children make sheep of their own. Materials you will need are one empty thread spool per child, cotton, white construction paper, glue, crayons, and scissors.

Glue cotton all around the spool. Have the head and tail sections of each sheep cut out ahead of time. Add details with crayons. Your older children can do much of this for themselves, but young preschoolers will need help. They can glue the heads and tails on the spools.

Spool-Sheep Fun

After the spool sheep are completed, let each child have a turn to hide his sheep and have the rest of the family search for it. He should "baaaa" when someone gets close to his sheep. A little one will not be able to do this, but will need an adult's help.

Close your Family Night by talking about how we can help other people by telling them of the love of God and Jesus.

Reading Time

Along with the love of God and Jesus, talk about their care for us, just as the shepherd cared for his sheep. Find some storybooks that illustrate this concept. *God Loves Us, God Loves Everybody, House Full of Prayers,* and *Saying Thank You Makes Me Happy* are all books that can be used for this purpose. Look at the pictures and talk about how God and Jesus care for people. "God cares for us by giving us food. . . . God hears us when we pray. . . . Jesus loves Grandma, brother, and so forth." Get the children to participate by asking them questions and having them answer or just point to pictures.

Patterns for spool sheep

UNIT 2: A Love of Jesus

ALWAYS SAY "THANK YOU"

GOAL
To help family members feel thankful to God and Jesus, and to lead them to express that thankfulness

BIBLE WORDS
"We . . . give thanks to God" (2 Thessalonians 1:3).

FAMILY ACTIVITIES

The Story of the Ten Lepers

Cut out the finger puppets on pages 71 and 75. You may want to color them before you cut them out.

The Bible tells us about some men who were very sick (Luke 17:11-19). There were ten sick men *(let the children help you count as you put on the ten finger puppets).*

Jesus came into the town where the ten sick men lived. The sick men called to Jesus, "Jesus, please help us. Make us well!"

Jesus saw the sick men. He loved them. He made them well. The men were so happy that Jesus had made them well. The men hurried away to tell their friends. *(Remove all but one puppet. Add Jesus puppet.)*

But one man did not hurry away. He came back to say thank-you to Jesus. Jesus was glad the man came back to say thank-you. *(Have puppet bow.)*

(Although there were nine unthankful men, do not emphasize this to preschoolers. A positive lesson will do far more good than a negative one.)

Next, let your children act out the story with the puppets. Let one child wear the ten puppets and another be Jesus. Then trade until everyone has had an opportunity to be Jesus and the ten sick men. There is no need to go into detail about leprosy. Preschoolers are not ready for this.

Discuss:
—Why do you think that just one man came back?
—How do you think Jesus felt when the nine men did not say thank-you? (Skip this one if your children are all quite young.)
—Why is it important to thank Jesus for what He has done for us?

—What are some things we can thank Jesus for now?

Thank-You Poster

Have a large piece of poster board, or a piece of butcher paper or something similar. Ahead of time, cut pictures from magazines or catalogs that show things we can thank God and Jesus for. Or, let the older children cut the pictures and the younger ones glue them on the poster. Print the words "Thank You, Jesus, for . . ." Include a picture of the Bible, and a church building. Keep the poster where everyone can see it in the coming week.

End with a time of thankfulness as each person has an opportunity to thank God and Jesus for at least one specific thing or person.

Thank-You Song

JESUS LOVES CHILDREN

GOAL

To help your children realize that Jesus loves all the children and is their friend

BIBLE WORDS

"You are My friends" (John 15:14).

FAMILY ACTIVITIES

How Do I Know Jesus Loves Me?

Start this Family Night by asking your children how they know that Jesus loves them.

After they have had time to express themselves, ask them for a song that tells them this. Of course they will know the answer to that! Then sing "Jesus Loves Me."

Ask, "How does this song say we know?" The answer is obvious, but it is good reinforcement for preschoolers.

Let your children sing "Jesus Loves the Little Ones Like Me," and "Jesus Loves the Little Children of the World."

Jesus Took Time for the Children

If you have the book *My Friend Jesus,* or another one that tells about Jesus and the children, read this to your children. If not, tell the story.

One day Jesus was teaching a group of people. Some mothers brought their children to see Jesus. Jesus' friends said, "Go away. Jesus is too busy to see your children."

But Jesus said, "Bring your children to me. I have time for them." The mothers brought their children close to Jesus. Jesus held them and put His arms around them. Jesus loved the children (Mark 10:13-16).

Discuss:

—How do we know Jesus loves children from this story?

—How do you think the children felt when Jesus touched them?

—How would you have felt if you had been one of the children with Jesus?

—What would you have said to Jesus?

"Jesus Loves Me" Book

Have your children make a "Jesus Loves Me" book. Fold two pieces of typing paper in half. Punch two holes and tie together with ribbon or yarn. Print the title on the front page. Glue a picture of Jesus on the cover.

Next, look for or draw pictures of things that remind us that Jesus loves us. For example, a house, food, parents, toys, animals, and so forth.

Thank Jesus for each of the things in the pictures as you work, or when you are finished.

Puzzles

Jesus Loves Little Children is an inlay puzzle with just a few pieces to put in place. Even toddlers can do this. *Jesus Loves the Little Children* (Frances Hook art) is planned for older preschoolers. Puzzles improve eye-hand coordination, and afford parents and teachers an opportunity to talk to the child as he is actively involved.

Role Play

This is a good story to role play. Set up a picture of Jesus, then let your children take some doll "children" to see Him. Sing the song below as the children walk.

Come to Me

S. T.   SYLVIA TESTER

"Come to me!" Je-sus said. "Hap-py chil-dren, come to me!"

THE GREAT TEA PARTY

GOAL
To help the family understand that Jesus wants all kinds of people to believe in Him and love Him

BIBLE WORDS
"Believe in the name of His Son Jesus Christ" (1 John 3:23).

FAMILY ACTIVITIES
Find a suitable tree for climbing and let your children have some fun. If you have a very small preschooler, just hold him on a low branch. While having your tree fun, tell the story of Zaccheus (Luke 19:1-10).

Let each child have a turn being Zaccheus. Let another family member be Jesus and say, "Come down, Zaccheus. I'm going to your house for tea." If you cannot go outside for this, use a stepladder or just a step stool in place of a tree. Children have good imaginations. They'll accept a substitute tree.

Sing a Song
Have the family sing the song "Zaccheus."

Zaccheus

① Hands in front, right palm raised above left palm. ② Bring palms a little closer together.
③ Alternate hands in climbing motions. ④ Shade eyes with right hand and look down.
⑤ "Walk" fingers of right hand up left forearm. ⑥ Shade eyes with right hand and look up.
⑦ Words are spoken, while looking up and shaking finger in admonition. ⑧ Clap hands on accented beat.

Tea Party
Have a special tea party with pretty cookies and a suitable substitute for tea. If possible, use your children's toy dishes.

As you eat, talk about the Bible story. Explain that tax collectors were not liked by most people because they took the people's money. But this didn't matter to Jesus. He loved Zaccheus and knew Zaccheus needed Him. Remind the children that everyone needs to hear about Jesus and become His friend. We must tell others so they will know Jesus and believe in Him.

Building Blocks
If your children have building blocks, have some fun with these. Show the children how to stack up a tall "tree" like the one Zaccheus climbed. Or, if they are able to build more complicated things, build Zaccheus' house and a road leading to it. Let them pretend to be Zaccheus and Jesus walking down the road to the house. Ask questions such as, "What do you suppose Zaccheus gave Jesus to eat? What would you have said to Jesus if you had been Zaccheus? . . . Would you like to have Jesus visit here?"

THE MYSTERY OF THE EMPTY TOMB

GOAL
To help family members experience together the joy of the resurrection of Jesus

BIBLE WORDS
"He is not here, for He has risen" (Matthew 28:6).

FAMILY ACTIVITIES
If your children are very young, and you feel that talking about Jesus' death might upset them, you would be wise to skip this Family Night program and simply take time to read some of their favorite Bible storybooks, work some puzzles together, sing familiar songs, and so forth. Make it a happy time together because our friend Jesus is alive! Go over the Bible Words with them.

Have fun making some play dough and using it together before you have a favorite dessert.

If you plan to talk about the death of Jesus, tell the story briefly like this:

Jesus loved everyone, but not everyone loved Jesus. In fact, some people hated Jesus! They did not like the good things He did. They did not believe that Jesus is the Son of God.

Some of these people who did not love Jesus had Him put on a cross, and Jesus died there. When Jesus was dead, His friends put His body in a tomb in the rocks, and put a large stone in front of the tomb.

But that's not the end of our story. Early on the first day of the week, some of Jesus' friends went to the tomb. When they looked inside, Jesus' body was not there. An angel told them, "Jesus is not here. He is alive!" Jesus' friends were excited! They ran to tell others.

Many of Jesus' friends saw Him after He was made alive. How happy they all were! Their friend Jesus was alive.

A Drama of the Empty Tomb
If your family enjoys drama, this story is a good one to present.

Use a large appliance box to represent the tomb. Have someone be the angel, and two or three to go to the tomb. Have them hurry to tell others that Jesus is alive.

Draw and Discuss
If your children are old enough, let them draw a mural of the resurrection scene. Give them a long piece of paper and crayons. It might be helpful to have a picture of the resurrection to help them get started.

As they work, discuss the following:
—Why did some people want to kill Jesus?
—How did Jesus' friends feel when He died?
—What did Jesus' friends see when they went to His tomb?
—How did Jesus' friends feel when they knew He was alive?
—How do we feel when we think about Jesus' being alive?

Take time for a prayer circle. Have each person thank God that Jesus is alive. Help your toddler to say "Thank You, God, for Jesus."

We Thank You, God in Heaven

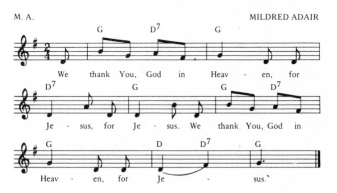

M. A.   MILDRED ADAIR

We thank You, God in Heav-en, for Je-sus, for Je-sus. We thank You, God in Heav-en, for Je - sus.

GOD'S WORLD IS BEAUTIFUL

GOAL
To help family members appreciate the beautiful world God has given us to enjoy

BIBLE WORDS
"God . . . made the world and all things in it" (Acts 17:24).

FAMILY ACTIVITIES
This would be a good night to go to a park. Take all the materials you will need to do the activities.

God's Beautiful World
Find pictures of as many of the following as possible: moon, stars, sun, lakes, streams, waterfalls, ocean, animals, flowers, birds, fish, mountains, trees, and people. Also have a sheet of black paper. Tell your family about creation.

Once there was a time when there was nothing. *(Show the black paper.)* Then God created a beautiful world for us to live in. *(Show all the pictures.)* He made all of these things for us to enjoy. After He made all this, He looked at the world and said, "It is good." Then He made people who could enjoy this wonderful world.

Have each family member choose his favorite picture. Let him tell why it is his favorite.

Play a Game
Play a game with four or five of the simplest pictures. Place them on the ground or on a table in front of everyone. When everyone hides his eyes, remove one picture from the group. Then let the family guess which picture is missing.

Another game to play while enjoying the beauty God created is "I See." Start by saying, "I see something God has made. The color of it is . . ." Of course, very young preschoolers will not be able to play this.

Nature Walk
Whether you are in a park, or at home, you can take a nature walk to look for beautiful things God has made. Explain that each person must look up (at trees, sky, etc.), look down (for pretty flowers, insects, stones), and look around. Each person is to find beautiful things God has made.

Nature Collage
Give each family member a paper bag. Each person is to pick up small objects along the way (stones, bark, pinecones, sticks, moss, leaves, etc.) to make a nature collage. When you return home give each one a piece of construction paper and some glue. Each person is to glue the objects he has found on the piece of construction paper.

Or, if you prefer, make this a family project. Use a piece of wood, perhaps an old weathered piece. Glue the objects on the wood after deciding the most pleasing arrangement. Hang this in the family room or kitchen where all can see it.

As you are doing this activity, talk about the many beautiful things God has given us to enjoy. Talk about some of the beautiful things you saw while you were walking together.

When family members have completed their collages, they may display their handiwork.

Action Rhyme
Do this action rhyme several times. Preschoolers love repetition!

God Has Made Everything Beautiful

God's world is beautiful.
  (Make a large circle with hands.)
God gave us beautiful mountains.
  (Put fingertips together to form mountain peaks.)
God gave us beautiful flowers.
  (Pretend to hold a flower and smell it.)
God gave us beautiful rivers.
  (Wiggle fingers like a rippling brook.)
God gave us beautiful trees.
  (Look up, hold up arms.)
Thank You, God, for Your beautiful world.
  (Fold hands and bow head.)

Dessert
Try some natural foods from God's beautiful world. Enjoy an assortment of nuts, dried fruits, sunflower seeds, and so forth.

TAKE CARE OF MY EARTH

GOAL

To make each family member aware that he is responsible for taking care of the beautiful world God has given him

BIBLE WORDS

"The earth He has given to the sons of men" (Psalm 115:16).

FAMILY ACTIVITIES

Remember God's Beautiful World

Review last week's Family Night. Talk about some of the beautiful things you saw on your walk. Or review by looking at magazine pictures of beautiful things created by God.

How Can We Keep God's World Beautiful?

Explain that God has made this beautiful world but He has told us we must take care of it (Genesis 1:27, 28; 2:15).

Find some pictures of how man has polluted God's beautiful earth. Discuss how your family can help keep God's earth beautiful. Include not only cleaning it up, but planting flowers, watering them, pulling weeds, raking leaves, and any other job you do in your yard.

Who Is Obeying?

Tell your children you are going to tell them two stories about children. They are to tell you which children are obeying God and keeping His earth beautiful, and which children are disobeying by not taking care of God's world.

Story #1: Danny and Susie walked to the park together. Danny's mother had given them each a stick of gum. They unwrapped their gum and threw the paper on the ground. Susie said, "It's OK to throw the gum wrappers on the ground. Someone will pick them up."

Story #2: Debbie and Johnny were playing on the sidewalk in front of their house. Their mother had given them some candy. They unwrapped their candy and put the paper in their pockets. Then Johnny saw a gum wrapper on the sidewalk. "Look," he said. "Someone threw down some paper. It looks bad! I want God's world to be beautiful." Johnny picked up the paper. Then he walked to the back of the house and threw the gum wrapper in the trash can.

Discuss:
—Which of the children obeyed God?
—Which children did not obey God?
—Why is it important always to put paper in a trash can?
—What are some ways we can help keep God's world beautiful? (See what the children remember of the earlier discussion.)

Project

Decide on a family project to help keep God's world beautiful. There may be some part of your neighborhood that looks trashy. Clean it together. (Make sure that preschoolers don't get hurt on the trash!)

Another idea is to take a family walk around your own yard. Have each person pick up any trash he may find and throw it away. For the benefit of the little ones, ahead of time "plant" several pieces of newspaper or something they can pick up.

If the weather permits, let the children plant seeds or plants in your yard, then encourage them to continue caring for them. Or, if it is winter, let the children plant seeds in an egg carton to be tended indoors until time to set the little plants outdoors. Make sure the children water the seeds and plants sufficiently.

Dessert

Have your dessert while you take your walk. Have something the children must unwrap. This will give them the experience of unwrapping and discarding the wrapper for themselves.

GOD CREATED ANIMALS

GOAL
To help family members be thankful for the animals God has made

BIBLE WORDS
"God made the beasts of the earth" (Genesis 1:25).

FAMILY ACTIVITIES
Start Family Night by reading or telling the story about God's creating the animals (Genesis 1:24, 25; 2:19, 20).

Find the Animals
Cut out pictures of as many animals as you can find. (Use the ones from the story of Noah, if you have them.) Hide them throughout the house. Tell your children you are going to have an animal hunt. Tell them to look carefully to see how many animals they can find.

After the animal hunt is over, sit on the floor and have your children give the names of the animals they have found. Toddlers may be able to make the sound the animal makes. Have each child hold up his favorite animal and tell why he likes the animal.

Have each person thank God for the animals He has made.

Add-a-Verse Song
To the tune below, sing about several of God's animals. Let your children suggest animals to use.

Crazy Animal Names
God told Adam to name the animals. If God were to ask you to name the animals, what would you call them? Hold up the animal pictures and have a good time giving the animals crazy names.

Play a simple game with your young preschooler. First, hold up pictures of common animals your little one is apt to recognize. Help him make the sound the animal makes. Then make the sound and let him hunt through the pictures spread on the floor to find the appropriate animal. Or, play a game that is a bit more complicated by saying, "I know an animal God made that goes 'oink' (or 'moo,' etc.). What is its name?" or, "Find the picture of the animal."

Dessert
Have another animal hunt. This time, hide animal crackers and let the children find them. Or, if you prefer a more elaborate dessert, decorate a cake or cupcakes by standing animal crackers on top or around the sides.

Books and Games
There are many interesting games and books about animals. Here are a few: games—*Bible Animal Dominoes, Noah's Ark Lotto*; sewing cards—*Bible Animals*; books—*God's Animals, God Made Puppies, God Made Kittens*.

God's World

J. M. G.   JOY M. GREWELL

God made ap - ples, God made ap - ples;
(dog - gies)   (dog - gies)
(flow - ers)   (flow - ers)

God made a won-der-ful world for me!

GOD MADE PETS

GOAL
To help children appreciate the fact that God had children in mind when He created certain animals that could be pets

BIBLE WORDS
"Oh give thanks to the Lord, for He is good" (Psalm 106:1).

FAMILY ACTIVITIES
Tell the following story to your children:

Brian lived on a farm. His dad kept lots of animals on the farm. There were horses, cows, chickens, pigs, dogs, and cats. Brian had a horse of his own called Star. Brian loved Star and Star loved Brian. Brian also had a dog named Shep. He was a very big dog.

One day Brian's daddy said, "Brian, we are going to move from our farm to the city. I have a new job."

"But Daddy," cried Brian, "what will happen to our animals? What will happen to Star and Shep?"

"Brian, I'm afraid we'll have to sell all the animals. Star and Shep are too big for the city," explained Daddy.

Brian ran to the barn, crying. Star and Shep were his best friends. How could he leave them?

Brian was sad every day. He didn't feel like playing. He didn't even feel like eating.

One day at dinner Brian's daddy said, "Brian, I know you are sad about losing Star and Shep. So am I. But we must learn to accept this move. Let's ask God to help us learn to get over losing our animals."

So Brian and Mommy and Daddy prayed that God would help them make the move to the city.

One day Brian's Aunt Mary came to visit. She said, "Brian, my dog Fluffy just had puppies. One puppy looks just like Fluffy. It is small, and has white hair that almost covers its eyes. Would you like to have this puppy?"

"Oh, yes!" said Brian. "I know I will love Fluffy's puppy. Thank you!"

Brian closed his eyes and said, "Thank You, God, for my new puppy. And thank You for helping me move to the city."

Discuss:
—Why did Brian feel sad?
—What did Brian's daddy say he should do?
—How did God answer Brian's prayer?
—Does God always give us everything we ask for?

Conclude by saying that God must have had children in mind when he made animals that can be pets. If you have pets in your family, take time to thank God for them.

Pet Show
Let your children put on a pet show for you. Suggest that they show their pet and tell why that pet is special. Have the pet do a trick.

If your children don't have a pet, let them have a pet show using stuffed animals. Have ribbons or prizes for all pets or stuffed animals. Use your imagination to think of categories. Leave no one out!

Remind the children that God expects them to take good care of their pets. Review rules you have made for the caring of pets.

Pet Scrapbook
Provide notebook paper, ribbon, scissors, glue, and magazines. Let the children cut pictures of pets from the magazines and glue them on the notebook paper. Tie together with ribbon. Write on the cover, "My Favorite Pets."

As everyone works, talk about the wonderful animals God has made.

Pet Store Trip
You might want to take your family to a pet store to look at the animals. Children always love this. Of course, they will want a new pet or two!

If you do not have a pet, perhaps this would be a good time to decide on a suitable one.

Puzzle and Book Fun
The puzzle, *We Are Helpers,* would be fun for your little one to work while the older children are finishing the scrapbooks or preparing for the pet show. You can talk to him about caring for a pet, and remind him that God made pets for us to enjoy.

Again read *God Made Puppies* and *God Made Kittens* if you have these books.

GOD MADE WATER

GOAL
To help family members see that God made water for us to use and enjoy

BIBLE WORDS
"God . . . made the world and all things in it" (Acts 17:24).

FAMILY ACTIVITIES
If you are fortunate enough to be near an ocean or lake, have your Family Night there. Start with a treasure hike.

Treasure Hike
Give each family member a container to put his treasures in. Encourage the children to look for shells, interesting rocks, pieces of wood, starfish, sand dollars, and whatever is available. After your hike, sit down and have each person show his treasures. Take time to thank God for the treasures He has given us to enjoy at the beach.

Sand Castles
Build a family sand castle. Let your children design the castle. Help only if you are asked. Talk about the fact that God made the ocean or lake and the sand.

While you rest, read the Genesis 1 account of creation, at least through verse 10. Talk about the uses for water, both functional and for fun.

ALTERNATE PLAN
If you cannot go to the ocean or to a lake, you can still have fun at home with this subject.

Make a Mural
Roll out a large sheet of newsprint. Draw a body of water with sand at the bottom, as shown in the sketch. Next, let the children color the water and sand.

On page 77 you will find pictures of things usually found at the beach. Cut these out and hide them throughout the house. Tell your children you are going to pretend you are at the beach. Explain that you are going for a walk around the house and each person must look for things that might be found at a beach.

When all pictures have been found, go back to the mural. Ask your children to name each object found and point on the mural where it belongs (sand, water, sky). Then let them glue the pictures in place. The children could color the pictures before gluing them to the mural.

As the child places the picture on the mural, say together, "Thank You, God, for the _____."

Hang the completed mural on the wall.

Water Fun
For the benefit of a young preschooler, put some water in a dishpan and have some floating toys to play with. Tell the child that God made the water for our use, then help him think of uses. As you play, very simply say, "Thank You, God, for water." Children need to learn that we can talk to God whenever we feel like it.

Also have shells for all the children to feel and look at, if possible.

Fish for Dessert
End this fun time by fishing for dessert. Hang a blanket in a doorway. Tie a clothespin to the end of a 4-foot piece of string. Tie the string to a stick to complete the fishing pole. Let your children toss the "hook" over the blanket. Put a piece of candy or other suitable Family Night treat on the "hook."

GOD MADE SEASONS

GOAL
To help family members see that God created seasons for them to enjoy

BIBLE WORDS
"He [God] . . . gave you rains from heaven and fruitful seasons" (Acts 14:17).

FAMILY ACTIVITIES
This Family Night is about seasons. God has given us four beautiful seasons to enjoy. To help you explain about the seasons, cut pictures from magazines to represent each season.

Summer—The season when it is very warm and lots of food is growing.

Autumn—The season when leaves fall from trees, when days start getting cooler.

Winter—The season when it becomes very cold.

Spring—The season when flowers and other things begin to grow; days become longer and warmer.

Read Genesis 8:22. God says we will always have the seasons to enjoy.

Game of the Seasons
Make a drawing of each of the symbols for the seasons. Give each child (or each family member) a drawing. Explain how to play the game. You will call off a word or phrase that particularly fits with one of the seasons. The child who has the drawing should hold it up and call out the name of the season. If you have a very young preschooler, someone older will need to help him play the game. Suggested words or phrases to call:

> vacation
> snow
> swimming
> picnic
> Christmas
> hot
> cold
> watermelon
> 4th of July
> school
> Easter
> Thanksgiving
> colorful leaves

Things Our Family Can Do
Ask your children for ideas on what they would like to do in the coming season. Make a list. Be creative. Plan some things you have never done before. If the season is summer, plan some Family Nights outdoors.

Mural of the Seasons
Roll out a large section of newsprint or butcher paper on the floor (enough for a two-foot section for each person). Have family members draw a picture of their favorite family activity for a given season. For younger children, draw an outline for them to trace with crayon, or glue pictures cut from magazines. Do not leave the little ones out.

Pray
Have each person thank God for the season he likes best, or for the season now in progress.

The Candy Tree
If you did not make a candy tree during unit 1, you may want to do one now.

Read a Book
If you have one, read a book on a season, such as *Thank You, God, for Winter; Thank You, God, for Spring; Thank You, God, for Summer;* and *Thank You, God, for Fall.*

GOD'S BOOK IS SPECIAL

GOAL
To make family members aware of the importance of God's Word, that it is a special book

BIBLE WORDS
"I shall not forget Thy [God's] word" (Psalm 119:16).

FAMILY ACTIVITIES
Have the children's Bible along with other books such as children's storybooks, a cookbook, a magazine or two, a dictionary, and so forth, on a table or on the floor. Then begin by telling the children that books are very important. Pick up various books and explain why they are important. Then tell them there is one Book that is more important than all the rest. By now they will know it is the Bible.

Tell the children about the boy Timothy whose mother, Eunice, and grandmother, Lois, read to him from God's Word. Mention the fact that, when Timothy became a man, he went everywhere telling others that God loved them and sent His Son, Jesus, to love them.

Sing a Song
To the tune of "Mulberry Bush," sing these words: "The Bible is a special book, a special book, a special book, etc., because it is God's Word." Set the Bible on a chair and make a circle around it as you sing.

Recording Session
Use a tape recorder tonight as you sing several of the children's favorite songs. Let them "read" the Bible Words and say anything else they want, then have fun listening. Children (and adults) enjoy hearing themselves on tape. Taping a storybook is another enjoyable experience for children.

Bible Puzzle Hunt
Ahead of time, make a construction-paper Bible (*see sketch*). Mount this on corrugated cardboard and cut into three or four pieces. Hide these pieces around the house. When the children need a little action, let them hunt for the pieces and see how quickly they can put the puzzle together. You will probably have to help a toddler. Remind them that they are looking for pieces of the best book of all—the Bible.

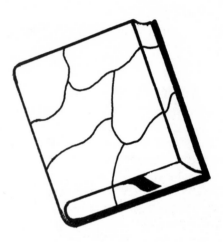

Have Fun
Learn this action rhyme to use tonight and other nights.

My Bible
This is my Bible;
   (Hands held out in front; palms together.)
I'll open it wide;
   (Open hands; but keep them touching.)
And see (or say) what is written
   On the inside!
   (Say Bible verse together.)
            —*Jean Baxendale*

BIBLE STORIES ARE TRUE

GOAL

To help your family realize that the Bible is true, and to help them enjoy Bible stories

BIBLE WORDS

"The words of the Lord are pure words" (Psalm 12:6).

FAMILY ACTIVITIES

Tonight we are going to talk about God's special book, the Bible. What does the Bible tell us? (Your children will probably answer by naming specific Bible stories.)

Favorite Bible Story Book

Give each family member five pieces of notebook paper. On the cover have them draw a picture of Jesus. If you have pictures of Jesus from Sunday-school papers you may want to glue these on the cover.

On the next four pages have family members draw pictures of their favorite Bible stories.

For a young preschooler, provide pictures cut from old take-home papers for him to glue in his book.

When this project is finished, have each person show and tell about his "Favorite Bible Story Book."

Conclude by talking about the Bible. Stress that the stories are true—they actually happened many years ago. This is an important concept for young children to learn and accept. You will go into other aspects of God's Word in future weeks.

Make sure that you have the Bible words highlighted and that everyone has a chance to "read" them.

Reading Time

Tonight is the ideal time to read several Bible storybooks. Make sure that the books are Scripturally accurate and written on the preschool level. (Short, simple sentences; preschool vocabulary; simple, uncluttered art; no symbolism.) *My Bible Book* was written specifically for young preschoolers in language they will understand. *The Very Best*

Book of All is a good book to read to older pre-schoolers, or have beginning readers read themselves. *Bible Stories Make Me Happy* offers a variety of Bible stories that are children's favorites.

Bible Song

This song can be used with many of the children's favorite stories by using the name of the main character at the end of each line.

The Bible

S. T.   SYLVIA TESTER

Here is the Bi - ble. The Bi - ble tells of Je - sus. God.

Here is the Bi - ble. The Bi - ble tells of Je - sus. God.

Dessert

If you have time to be a bit creative, bake a cake and decorate it to look like a Bible, either open or closed.

WE LEARN FROM THE BIBLE

GOAL

To help family members realize that God wants us to know His Word and follow it

BIBLE WORDS

"Blessed [happy] are they that hear the word of God, and keep it" (Luke 11:28, KJV).

FAMILY ACTIVITIES

Young children need to know that rules are part of life. They also need to know that rules are given out of love and concern. To begin Family Night, tell about the giving of the Ten Commandments.

God's people had been walking and walking. God was leading them to a new place. Moses was the leader God had given His people. They came to a very big mountain, called Mt. Sinai.

God told Moses to have the people camp at the foot of Mt. Sinai. God told Moses to get the people ready for something very special. The people were to wait at the foot of the mountain.

A big cloud came over the top of the mountain. Thunder crashed! The mountain shook! The people were afraid! Then Moses went to the top of the mountain.

God spoke to Moses while he was on the mountaintop. He gave Moses rules for His people to live by. He did this because He loved His people and wanted them to be happy. If they followed the rules they would be happy.

Moses took the laws, written on two large stones, down to the people. Moses said, "These are God's special rules. If you follow them you will be happy."

Discuss:
—Who was the leader of God's people?
—Where did the people stay?
—Where did Moses go?
—What did God give Moses?
—Why did God give His people rules?
—Do we have rules to follow?

Safety Rules

Let the children help you make a traffic light. Cover a milk carton with black construction paper.

Cut 4 red circles, 4 yellow, and 4 green, and glue them in place. While you work, talk about the importance of following safety laws or rules. Mention such rules as looking both ways before crossing the street, not running across the street, and not riding bikes in traffic. Make sure your children know that these rules are made for their protection.

If the weather is good, let the children take the traffic light outside and use it as they ride their bikes or other vehicles. Or, use it indoors with toy cars and trucks. If you have building blocks, have fun building a city. Make sure that everyone obeys traffic rules. If your children are in the habit of having violent crashes as they play cars, now would be a good time to encourage them to be safe drivers. Children need to learn to play creatively, not violently.

Simon Says

The old game, "Simon Says," illustrates following rules. Play this with older children. Little ones will have a difficult time, unless you make the rules clear and keep the commands very simple. If little ones play with you, don't make them stay out of the game if they don't "obey." They will lose interest.

Play Games

Play a table game or two that your preschoolers enjoy. Stress the importance of following the rules.

Books

A Child's Book of Manners; Buzzy Bee Says, "Be Happy"; Buzzy Bee Story Book; Obedience; and *Honesty* all carry out the theme of obeying rules. Read at least one book tonight. Preschoolers love to be read to!

Dessert

Serve finger gelatin cut in the shape of the stone tablets. Here is a recipe for the gelatin:
   4 small packets of unflavored gelatin
   3 small boxes of flavored gelatin
   4 cups boiling water
Stir boiling water into gelatin until gelatin and sugar are dissolved. Pour into large, flat cake pan. Refrigerate until solid. Cut into shapes desired.

THE BIBLE TELLS ABOUT JESUS

GOAL
To help family members know that the Bible tells us about Jesus, and to lead them to be thankful for Jesus

BIBLE WORDS
"Jesus is the Christ, the Son of God" (John 20:31).

FAMILY ACTIVITIES
Start out the evening with a period of discussion on Bible facts about Jesus. Let your children tell all they can think of about Jesus. You may need to ask a few questions to get them started. Remind them of some of the well-known Bible stories about Jesus or that He told. Of course, young preschoolers will be unable to tell you much. Try to have some pictures of Jesus to look at. Ask your toddler who is in the picture, or ask him to point to his friend Jesus. One Bible fact most tiny ones will know is "Jesus loves me!" What an important fact to know! You may want to have a book, such as *Jesus Makes Me Happy,* to show pictures from Jesus' life. *My Friend Jesus* is written on a young preschool level and will be a help in discussing Jesus with your little ones. Make sure that the Bible is included in your books and help the little ones "read" the Bible words.

Bible-Facts Book
Make a "Bible Facts About Jesus" book with your children. Put several pages together into a book and let your children choose pictures (from old take-home papers) to glue into the book. On each page print such facts as "Jesus is the Son of God,"

"Jesus loves me," "Jesus made sick people well," "Jesus taught the people," and so forth. Help the children find pictures that fit with your statements. When the book is complete, read it together, then keep it available throughout the week. If your preschooler is quite young, cover the pages with clear, adhesive-backed plastic so they won't tear.

Puzzles and Books
Have a period of play with your children. Provide appropriate puzzles and books and let them choose what they want to do.

Make Some Music
Since there are so many songs about Jesus for little ones, sing some of these tonight. One used previously, "The Bible" (page 39), would be quite appropriate tonight. Rhythm instruments, ready-made or improvised, are fun for preschoolers.

GOD LISTENS WHEN WE PRAY

GOAL
To help family members understand that God always hears our prayers

BIBLE WORDS
"We know that He [God] hears us" (1 John 5:15).

FAMILY ACTIVITIES

Paul and Silas in Jail

Paul and Silas were missionaries. That means they went everywhere telling people about Jesus. Many people were glad to know about Jesus. But some people were not glad. They did not want to know about Jesus and they did not want others to hear either. These people had Paul and Silas beaten and thrown in jail.

Paul and Silas had their feet fastened so they could not even stand up. What do you think they did while they were in jail? Were they angry? Did they cry? No. The Bible tells us that Paul and Silas sang songs to God and they prayed!

Stop and discuss:
—What do you think they sang?
—What did they pray about?
—How would you have felt if you were in their places?

All of a sudden, the jail began to shake. All the doors flew open. The chains fell off the prisoners' feet. They were free! Did Paul and Silas run away as fast as they could? No. They stayed and talked to the jailer. He and His family wanted to know about God and about Jesus.

A Prison Play

Have a family play about the story. Use a cardboard box with holes in it for the prisoners' feet. Tie hands if you wish.

Scene #1: Paul and Silas are beaten and thrown into jail.

Scene #2: Paul and Silas are singing and praying. The jail shakes and all the doors come open.

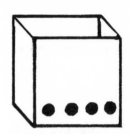

Scene #3: The jailer rushes in and wants to know about Jesus. (The fact that he is about to kill himself is not important or necessary for preschoolers. Also, "being saved" is not in their thinking yet. Simply state that Paul and Silas told him about Jesus. This they can understand.)

Does God Listen?

Discuss with your children about how God answers prayer. Assure them that He always listens. Remind them that there are several answers to our requests—yes, no, and later. Too often we stress only the yes answers we receive from God. Help your children understand that they will not always receive everything they ask God for. This doesn't mean that God isn't answering them. You may want to mention several instances where you feel God answered your prayers very directly.

Talk to God

Suggest that everyone take a turn praying to God "because we know God is listening to us."

Reading Time

I Learn to Pray will help your young preschooler understand prayer a little better. *House Full of Prayers* will show your older children the many instances they can talk to God throughout the day.

"I can pray for . . ."

Have each family member make an "I can pray for . . ." book. Use several sheets of construction paper folded in half. Punch holes and tie with yarn. On each page draw a picture of something or someone to pray for or about—family members, the church, a missionary, someone who is sick or shut-in, and so forth. Take time to pray for the ones in the books. Keep the books on display to remind each person of special prayer needs.

THANK YOU, LORD

GOAL
To help your family feel thankful for God's blessings and to learn to express that thankfulness

BIBLE WORDS
"Give thanks to Him" (Psalm 100:4).

FAMILY ACTIVITIES

Jesus Is Thankful
Briefly tell the story of Jesus and His apostles and the last supper. Although there is far more meaning to the entire passage, just dwell on the fact that Jesus gave thanks for the bread and juice. Here is the story in brief:

There was a time when Jesus and His helpers were going to eat a special supper together. Jesus' helpers prepared the meal.

Jesus told His friends, "I am glad we can have this meal together."

While Jesus and His helpers were eating the supper, Jesus said thank-you to God two times. First He said, "Thank You, God, for this juice." Then He said, "Thank You, God, for this bread."

Discuss:
—Who was eating with Jesus?
—What did Jesus do as they were eating?
—What did Jesus say thank-you for?
—What does this tell us?
—What else can we say thank-you for?

A "Tea Party"
Let your children help you prepare the dessert or snack for tonight. Then, have a special "tea party" for the dolls and/or stuffed animal friends. Take turns saying thank-you to God for the food. Also encourage everyone to use good manners and say thank-you to each other.

Thank-You Poster
Have a large poster board or sheet of paper, glue, and plenty of magazine or catalog pictures of things (or people) we should be thankful for. Print in large letters "We thank God ..." Even the youngest child can help add pictures. You may want to purchase a glue stick or glue roll-on for the little ones to use. Let the children hang the poster in their room after tonight.

When the poster is finished, or as you work on it, teach the simple song below to your family. Let them think of things to add, or add stanzas using the cut-out pictures for ideas.

We Thank You, Thank You, God

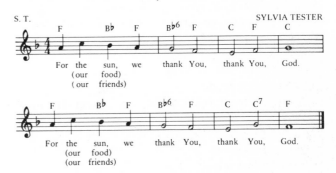

Guess What's Missing
Have everyone sit around the table. Have on display several objects or foods that you can be truly thankful for. While everyone has his eyes closed and covered, remove one object. Then let everyone guess what is missing. After a while, remove two items to keep the game interesting.

DANIEL PRAYED TO GOD

GOAL
To help family members see that God will give us courage to do what is right

BIBLE WORDS
"Seek the Lord and His strength" (Psalm 105:4).

FAMILY ACTIVITIES
Read from a Bible storybook, or tell the story of Daniel from Daniel 6. Keep the story simple, leaving out unnecessary details. Or, let your child or children tell the story. Give a few hints where necessary.

The Story in Song
To the tune of "Three Blind Mice," sing the story:

Daniel prayed to God
Daniel prayed to God
Three times a day,
Three times a day.
Three men were spying as Daniel prayed.
They told the king he had not obeyed.
In the lions' den he was not afraid.
'Cause Daniel prayed to God.

The Drama of Daniel
Place some chairs in a large circle and hang blankets on them. This is the lions' den. Next choose a family member to be Daniel and two family members to be lions. Have the lions go into the den and start roaring. Then have Daniel go into the den. The lions should become quiet and lie down as soon as Daniel gets into the den.

Next, have the king come and call for Daniel. He asks, "Has your God been able to save you?"

Daniel answers, "Yes, O King. He shut the mouths of the lions."

Discuss:
—Why did Daniel get thrown into the lions' den?
—How do you think Daniel felt?
—How would you have felt?
—Why was Daniel not harmed? (He trusted God.)
—Can you trust God the way Daniel did?

When the Lion Roars
Play a game of "When the Lion Roars." One person is the lion. He must wrap a blanket around himself and put a paper sack on his head (with eye holes of course). The rest of the family hides in the house. The lion must crawl from room to room until he finds all the family. When he finds a person he must roar. Then that person must go back to where you were having your Family Night and wait until the lion finds the rest of the family. All the children will want a turn at being the lion!

Take Time to Pray
Give everyone a paper plate, crayons or felt-tip pens, a paper fastener, and two hands for a clock. Show them how to make a clock face and put on the hands. You will have to help your young preschooler with this. Show by the clock hands when Daniel prayed to God. Talk about the times you can pray.

Encourage your children to talk about something that may be bothering them, or something they need courage for. Then take time to pray about these things. Remind them of Daniel's trust in God and the courage he received from God.

BUILDING
A POSITIVE RELATIONSHIP
WITH MYSELF

Unit 6: A Love of Myself

GOD GIVES US EYES

GOAL
To help family members become aware of God's wonderful gift to us—our eyes

BIBLE WORDS
"The seeing eye, the Lord has made" (Proverbs 20:12).

FAMILY ACTIVITIES

Blind Tag
Start by playing Blind Tag. Select one family member to be the "blindman." Blindfold that person. The rest of the family joins hands and tries to hop on one foot away from the blindman. The blindman must tag someone. The family member who is tagged then becomes the blindman. Confine the game to one room.

Discuss:
—How does it feel to be blind?
—Why does God give us eyes?
—What can we see?

Eyes, Eyes, Eyes
Make a poster of eyes. Look in magazines for pictures of eyes. Cut out the eyes and glue them on the poster. Print the Bible words at the top. Then talk to the family about eyes. Mention that God gives different colors of eyes, different shapes, and so forth. No two peoples' eyes are the same. Remind the children how hard it was to play the game used earlier. Talk about the ways we use our eyes as we work, play, study, drive, and so forth.

Looking Walk
If weather permits, take a "looking walk" outdoors. Before you start, tell the children you want them to watch for certain things along the way. As you walk, use the words "look at" and "see" or "use your eyes" frequently.

When you return from your walk, let the family members draw a picture of something they saw on their looking walk. Have some coloring pages ready for your small ones to scribble-color.

Look and Remember
Have everyone look around the room and become aware of what is there. Then have everyone close his eyes and tell what he remembers seeing. You will have to ask your young preschooler if he saw certain things.

Next, play a game of "I Spy." You need good eyes for this!

Look at Books
One of the most important ways we use our eyes is to read or look at books. Tonight get out books on the wonderful things God has made for us to enjoy looking at. Some appropriate ones are *God's Colors* and *God's World* for the young set, and *Thank You, God, for Wonderful Things; God's Beautiful World;* and *God's World of Colors* for older preschoolers.

Shapes and Colors
Have a number of shapes cut from construction paper. Cut the same shape in several colors. Give the children exercises in matching colors and shapes. First, put out two different shapes in the same color and have the children find a third shape in the matching *color.* Do this several times. Then put out two pieces cut in the same shape but in different colors. Have them match the *shape* in another color. You can also line up three identical shapes and one odd one for the children to pick the one that doesn't belong.

For a young child, show him a shape and have him pick out a matching one (only give him two to choose from at first, then add a third if he catches on). Make this a fun game and remind the children that they must use the eyes God gave them to find the right piece.

Dessert
Make a dessert that is not only good to eat but pleasing to look at.

GOD GIVES US EARS

GOAL
To help family members appreciate the wonderful gift of hearing God has given us

BIBLE WORDS
"The hearing ear . . . the Lord has made" (Proverbs 20:12).

FAMILY ACTIVITIES

Listening Walk
Explain to your family that they are about to go on a "listening walk" tonight. They must be very quiet and listen for certain sounds. The sounds to listen for are birds singing, the wind, cars, voices, footsteps, water running, and music. (*Add to this list, or omit those that will be impossible in your area.*) No one is to speak unless he hears one of the specific sounds.

Identifying Sounds
Use a cassette recorder to record many different sounds around your home. Here are suggestions for sounds to catch: water running, paper being crumpled, vacuum cleaner, doorbell, a dog barking, dishes and silverware being handled, and washing machine. Let the children guess what each sound is.

Our Wonderful Ears
Read the Bible words and let the children say them with you. Then discuss:
—Why did God give us ears?
—What would it be like if we didn't have ears?
—What couldn't we do?
Have each family member thank God for his ears.

Funniest/Scariest Sound
Let each family member hide behind something and make the funniest sound he can think of, then make the scariest sound. The rest of the family must try to guess what these sounds are supposed to be. Or, for the benefit of a young child, just laugh at the funniest and act appropriately frightened at the scary sound!

Color an Ear
Just for family fun draw a giant ear on a piece of butcher paper. Work together to make the most colorful ear in the world!

Listen to Others
We need to use the wonderful ears God has given us by listening to others. Here is an action rhyme you can learn together.

God Gave Me Ears
God gave me two ears so I can hear.
(Point to ears.)
I can hear my daddy,
(Point to Dad.)
I can hear my mommy.
(Point to Mom.)
I can hear my brothers and sisters.
(Point to siblings.)
When they speak I listen.
(Cup hand around ears.)
Thank You, God, for ears.
(Fold hands and look up.)

Music for Our Ears
What would music be without ears? Take time to sing lots of the children's favorite Bible music. Use your cassette recorder to catch the singing on tape, then let the kids listen to themselves. Use impromptu rhythm instruments. Let everyone find his own from ordinary things around the house.

Dessert
As you enjoy your dessert, play records of good music. Make the entire evening a celebration of sound!

UM-MMMMMM GOOD!

GOAL
To help family members appreciate the wonderful gift of taste God has given us

BIBLE WORDS
"God is good" (Psalm 73:1).

FAMILY ACTIVITIES
Share the following with your family:

What would it be like if everything tasted the same? Let's pretend that everything tastes like dirt. Now let's eat a candy bar. *(Everyone plays like he is eating a candy bar that tastes like dirt.)* Now let's eat some dirt ice cream. *(Everyone pretends to do this.)*

Wouldn't it be terrible if everything we ate tasted the same? It would be especially bad if it all tasted like dirt! But God made us so we can taste many flavors.

Discuss:
—What tastes can you think of? (sweet, sour, etc.)
—What are some things that taste sweet?
—What are some things that taste sour?
—What are some things that taste salty?
—What is a taste you don't like?
—What is your favorite taste?

Blindfold Taste-Test
Blindfold your children, one at a time, and let them taste several different kinds of cereal. See if they can tell what kind of cereal each is. If you prefer, let them taste several different liquids. Or, let them taste a variety of tastes—ham, pickles, apples, sugar, and so forth. Talk about the salty taste of the ham, etc., as they eat each thing.

Thank God for Taste
Read Proverbs 24;13—"My son, eat honey, for it is good, yes, the honey from the comb is sweet to your taste." Have some honey on the table for your children to sample. Ask the children what kind of taste the honey has. Discuss for a few minutes how God has given us bees so some of our food can taste sweet. If you know someone who has a bee-hive, a trip to see it would make your Family Night even more exciting.

Have each family member thank God for giving us a sense of taste so we can enjoy our food.

Make a Montage
Let the children make a montage of pictures of food cut from magazines. Try to include a variety of tastes. You could even include some actual foods to make this a collage. Print "Thank You, God, for our sense of taste."

Tasty Dessert
This is a good night for a tasty dessert. You may want to try something new for your family to taste.

Sing About Food
Use the song found on page 34 and let the children add as many stanzas as they want.

IT'S FUN TO FEEL!

GOAL
To help family members appreciate the sense of feeling God has given us

BIBLE WORDS
"God is good" (Psalm 73:1).

FAMILY ACTIVITIES
Jill and John are five-year-old twins. They have red hair and freckles. They love to play at the beach. Today they went to the beach with their mother and father. While Mom and Dad cooked hot dogs Jill and John ran off to play.

"Bury me in the sand," said John. So Jill began to cover him with sand. Soon all you could see were John's head and toes.

"You look silly," laughed Jill.

"The sand feels rough and makes me feel itchy," said John.

Next Jill and John ran to the water to wash off the sand. "Oh!" cried Jill. "The water feels cold and wet." Jill and John had fun running through the waves.

Jill and John were beginning to feel hungry. "We'd better go back for lunch," they said.

"Look at this," said John. "It looks like an icky vegetable."

"I wouldn't eat that," laughed Jill. "That's seaweed." She picked it up. It felt slimy.

"Look what I found," said Jill as she picked up a beautiful shell. "Feel how smooth it is."

John and Jill hurried back to where Mom and Dad were. Do you know who got there first? It was a tie.

"The food is about ready," said Daddy. "I'd better put some suntan lotion on you two before you get a sunburn."

"I think I'm already burnt a little," said John. "My back feels hot and sore."

"We sure feel a lot of different things at the beach," said Jill.

"Suppose you tell us about all these feelings while we eat," said Mother.

So Jill and John told Mom and Dad about the many things they had felt that day. "Isn't it good that God has given us a sense of feeling," said Dad. "Let's thank God for our sense of feeling."

Discuss:
—What different things did Jill and John feel?
—How did the sand feel? the water?
—How did the sun make John feel?
—How did the seaweed feel? the shell?

Feelings in a Bag
Put the following items in a paper bag: a piece of sandpaper, a smooth stone, a wet rag, an ice cube, and a marshmallow or cotton ball.

Let one child at a time put his hand in the bag to try to identify the objects without seeing them. Ask him to describe how each item feels.

Touch 'n Feel Book
For the benefit of your young preschoolers, make a touch 'n feel book. Put together several pieces of poster board, punched and tied with ribbon or yarn. On each page put one or more samples of textures—sandpaper, cotton, a piece of aluminum foil, a scrap of velour or velvet or corduroy, a twig and leaf, and so forth. Or, you could glue all these textured items on a large piece of poster board or cardboard and hang it on the wall.

More Touch 'n Feel
This would be a good night to do some finger painting. Use the recipe on page 69 to make your own finger paint. A slick shelf paper will work with this. Or, a simple way to finger-paint is to use dark construction paper and a non-menthol shaving cream. Little ones will love spreading and feeling this with their fingers. They won't make a picture of anything; they will just enjoy doing it.

Play dough is another good activity to use with a session on feelings. Squeezing, rolling, pulling, pounding, and shaping the pliable dough are all good feelings!

Dessert
See how many different textures you can combine for snacks tonight. Pretzels, marshmallows, jello, various crackers, raisins, and banana slices are a few foods with interesting textures.

OUR WONDERFUL BODIES

GOAL
To help family members appreciate the wonderful bodies God has given us

BIBLE WORDS
"I will give thanks to Thee, for I am . . . wonderfully made" (Psalm 139:14).

FAMILY ACTIVITIES

I Am Wonderfully Made
Explain to your family that this Family Night will be about the wonderful bodies God has given us.

On pages 79 to 85 you will find large cut-out pictures of boys and girls. You will notice, however, that these boys and girls must be assembled. Also, the faces are blank. If you need more girls or boys, use these as patterns and cut what you need.

Give each child a "paper child" to color and then cut out. You will need to cut for the very young child. Then help each child assemble his paper child by using paper fasteners.

Discuss:
—Why did God give us legs?
—Why did God give us arms and hands?
—Why did God give us a mouth, eyes, ears, etc.
—What would it be like if we didn't have some of these parts of the body (mouth, for example)?

Remind the children that God has given us just what we need. Then go over the Bible words several times with the children. See if anyone can say them by himself.

Now have a circle of prayer with each person thanking God for his wonderful body.

Here's How My Body Works
Have each person do something special with some part of his body. For example, someone may want to make a loud noise with his mouth, jump with his feet and legs, make a funny face, do an action rhyme with his hands and arms, do an exercise or trick using his entire body. Your young preschooler will need help with this.

Do Calisthenics
Tonight, use your entire bodies in some simple calisthenics. Start with a favorite of young children, to the tune of "Mulberry Bush": "Heads and shoulders, knees and toes, Knees and toes, knees and toes; Heads and shoulders, knees and toes, Clap your hands for Jesus!" (Do the obvious actions.) Go through a variety of actions, standing on one foot, jumping, bending, stretching, running in place, leg lifts, knee bends, and so forth. (You will probably tire of this before the kids do!)

If you want a less strenuous activity, do this action rhyme, pointing to the appropriate parts of the body as they are mentioned.

God Made Me

God made my eyes,
   God made my nose.
God made my fingers
   And all of my toes.

God made my ears,
   My mouth, my knee.
God made my feet
   And all of me.

I bow my head
   And bend my knee,
To say "Thank You, God,
   For making me."
    —Marian Bennett

Books
I'm Glad to Be Me, All About Hands, Busy Feet, and God Made Me are all excellent books for tonight's subject.

Dessert
Gingerbread men would be fun for dessert. Tell the story of the gingerbread man (use the book if you have it) as you eat.

UNIT 6: A Love of Myself

YOU ARE SPECIAL

GOAL
To help each family member understand that God has made him special

BIBLE WORDS
"God has made me" (Job 33:4).

FAMILY ACTIVITIES
Obtain a fairly large roll of paper for tonight's activities. Cut a sheet for each child, at least one foot longer than the child. Place the paper on the floor. Then have him lie down on the paper on his back. Trace around your child's body with a felt-tip pen or crayon. Give your child colored markers or large crayons to color in the details. You may have to draw these in for younger children and let them scribble-color. If you are helping a child, ask him what he wants you to do and what colors to use.

While you work together, talk about how special your child is, noticing the special way he is coloring himself. Several times during the project say "God has made you special. There is no one just like you!"

Hang the pictures of your children in a prominent place for the next week.

Look at Me!
One way to make a child feel special is to get out his baby pictures and look at them. Tell him how you took care of him, what he used to do, how cute he was, and so forth. This is particularly helpful if there is a bit of sibling rivalry, especially on the part of an older child who may resent the little one.

Squeaky Squirrel
Use the following story to help your children understand their own uniqueness.

Squeaky Squirrel was unhappy. "Mom," he said, "I wish I were like the other animals in the forest. They're better than I am."

"Why do you say that?" asked his mother.

"Well," Squeaky replied, "Barry Bunny can run faster than I can. Billy Beaver can build things better than I can. I'm just not as good as my friends. I wish I were someone else."

"Squeaky," his mother said lovingly, "you are very special and I love you just the way you are."

"What makes me special?" asked Squeaky.

"Many things," replied Squeaky's mother. "You are a squirrel, Squeaky. That means you are different from all the other forest animals. And that's good. It wouldn't be any fun if all the animals were exactly alike.

"You have a beautiful bushy tail. You have a lovely furry coat. You are also a very hard worker. And what's more important, you are kind. Remember last year, when Grandpa Squirrel was sick and couldn't work? You helped him store his food for the winter. That was very kind! Not many forest animals would do that. Yes, Squeaky, you are very special. I love you just because you're you!"

"Well, Mom," answered Squeaky happily, "I guess I am pretty special. I'm going to be happy with myself just the way I am!"

Discuss:
—What lesson did Squeaky learn?
—What made Squeaky special?
—What makes you special?
—Does God want you to like yourself?

Special Activity
Let your children suggest a fun activity they would like to do, perhaps a game that involves the entire family.

Books to Read
God Made Me; I'm Glad to Be Me; and Thank You, Lord, for Me all will help your children realize they are part of God's handiwork, and as such, very special indeed.

Dessert
Make a dessert that is a favorite of your children's. You probably already know what that is. Have plenty on hand!

TALENT NIGHT

GOAL
To help family members see that God has given everyone special talents and that talents can be used for God

BIBLE WORDS
"The Lord has made everything" (Proverbs 16:4).

FAMILY ACTIVITIES
God has given each of us special talents. It is important for us to help our children recognize and develop these talents. Before this Family Night ask each of your children to prepare something special for tonight. For instance, someone may sing a song, do a trick, tell a joke, stand on his head or do a somersault, draw a picture, tell a story, bake some cookies, put on a puppet show, and so forth. (Some of these would have to be done beforehand, of course.) Define *talent* for your children. Explain that a talent is something you can do well.

The Great Family Talent Show
Appoint someone to be the M.C. Make a big deal over each talent. Clap and cheer at the end of each great act. Your children may sense, when they see the response they get, that they are multi-talented and will offer to do several more acts for you!

At the end of the talent show talk about how special each person's talent was.

A Shepherd Boy With a Special Talent
Share the following Bible story with your family:

King Saul was feeling very bad. The king's servants said, "Music will help you feel better, King Saul. We will find someone to play the harp for you."

The servants knew there was a shepherd boy by the name of David who could play beautiful music on his harp.

When David played for the king the king did feel better for a time. David used his talent to help others.

Discuss:
—How did David use his talent?

—How can you use your talent to help others?
—How can you use your talent for God?

The Little Girl Without a Talent
Sharon was very sad. All of her friends had special talents. Bobby could run very fast. Heidi could sing. Jennifer could stand on her head and also do perfect cartwheels. Joey could draw good pictures.

"I can't do anything special," Sharon thought to herself. "I guess God didn't give me any talents."

That afternoon Sharon said to her mother, "Mommy, can I bake some cookies to take to Grandpa and Grandma? They like my cookies and it makes them happy when I go to see them."

"Of course you may," said Mother. "You are so kind to your grandma and grandpa."

Discuss:
—Why was Sharon sad?
—Did Sharon have a talent? (baking cookies)
—Did she have another talent? (making others happy)
—What would you tell Sharon to make her feel better?

Make a Harp
Let the children make little harps to remind them of David who used his talent to help others. Use the pattern on page 69. Cut these from heavy cardboard (poster board or corrugated cardboard). Cut notches where indicated. Let the children paint these with poster paint or color with crayons, then stretch rubber bands to fit in the notches. Or, if you prefer, punch holes and string yarn back and forth to make strings. Dip one end of each piece of yarn into white glue, twist and let dry. This will make a good point to put through the holes.

Dessert
Plan to have a dessert the children can help prepare. Comment on the fact that they used their talents to make the good dessert. Or, perhaps this can be Mommy's special talent for the evening.

BUILDING
A POSITIVE RELATIONSHIP
WITH OTHERS

Unit 7: A Love of My Family
Unit 8: A Love of Others

FAMILY FUN NIGHT

GOAL
To have fun as a family

FAMILY ACTIVITIES
Following are a variety of activities from which to choose. Select the activities your children will enjoy the most.

Spin the Bottle
If you have older preschool children and/or elementary-age children, play "Spin the Bottle." You will find situation cards on pages 87 to 93. Cut these apart. You may want to sort these into two piles, according to difficulty. You will also need a pop bottle.

Sit in a circle on the floor. Place the cards face down in a stack. Put the bottle in the middle of the circle. Have someone spin the bottle. Whoever it points to gets to draw a card. Read the card for your child and have him follow the instructions.

Use a kitchen timer to limit the game. Have fun!

Hide and Seek
Let one family member hide while someone counts to twenty. The entire family then tries to find the person who is hiding. Take turns.

Water Fight
If it is warm weather, have a water fight. Put on your swimsuits. Turn on the hose and fill containers with water. Have a good time!

Bucking Bronco
Each child gets to ride Dad, the "bucking bronco." Careful, Dad. This could be dangerous!

Family Wrestling Match
Everyone is on the floor at the same time. Just have a good time roughhousing.

Squat Tag
One person is selected to be it. He chases the others, but can't tag them when they squat.

Paper Planes
Show your children how to make paper airplanes. Have a contest to see whose plane will fly the farthest, the highest, and so forth.

Table Games
Let your children choose their favorite table game to play. You might even want to buy a new game for the occasion.

Balloon Soccer
Set up two goals. Divide the family into two teams. One team must kick the balloon past the other's goal to score a point. If your children are very young, just have fun kicking the balloon around the room.

Paper Dolls
Make your own paper dolls from cardboard and make clothes from colored paper. Or have fun cutting out paper-doll chains. Color these with crayons or felt-tip pens.

Read Books
Preschoolers need to vary quiet and active times. Have the children rest while you read their favorite storybooks to the entire family.

Picture Night
For another quiet activity, roll out a large piece of newsprint and have fun drawing and coloring pictures.

Family Circus
Get out all the stuffed animals. Have a family circus. Let each member have a turn doing an "act."

Prayer Circle
End your fun night on a serious note by having a prayer circle in which you thank God for the happy time with your family.

Fun Dessert
Plan on going to the store to let each person pick out his own dessert. You'd better set a limit!

OBEY YOUR PARENTS

GOAL
To help children know that God wants them to obey their parents and to talk about why it is important

BIBLE WORDS
"Children, obey your parents in the Lord" (Ephesians 6:1).

FAMILY ACTIVITIES

Bobby the Great

Bobby was four years old. He had a big smile, bright blue eyes, and curly hair. People would look at Bobby and say, "Isn't he cute! What a fine boy!"

Bobby could run faster and jump higher than any boy or girl in the neighborhood.

Bobby began to think, "I'm better than everyone else. I'm great!" Then he began to make fun of the other children. "Ha, ha," he would say. "You're not as good as I am. I'm Bobby the Great!"

Bobby's parents noticed what he was doing. "Bobby," Dad said, "it is not right for you to make fun of other children." But Bobby didn't listen.

Bobby ate candy when he wasn't supposed to. He stayed up to watch TV when he wasn't supposed to. "I don't have to obey my parents," thought Bobby, "because I'm Bobby the Great!"

One day Bobby decided to disobey his parents by crossing the street. He didn't look both ways to see if any cars were coming. He didn't need to. He was Bobby the Great! Cars could watch for him!

Suddenly Bobby heard brakes screech. The next thing he knew he was on the ground with a crowd around him. Bobby had been hit by a car!

Bobby was taken to a hospital in an ambulance. His parents sat with him and held his hand. Bobby was afraid! His leg hurt very bad!

The doctor who put his leg in a cast said, "Bobby, you are a lucky boy. You could have been killed. But you only have a broken leg. You must be more careful when you cross streets."

After the doctor left Bobby said to his parents, "I'm sorry I disobeyed you. I'm sorry I've been mean to my friends. I'm not Bobby the Great anymore. From now on I'm just plain Bobby."

The next day Bobby went home from the hospital. He had learned his lesson. From that time on Bobby tried to obey his parents and be nice to his friends.

Discuss:
—Why did Bobby call himself "Bobby the Great"?
—What did Bobby do wrong?
—What happened to Bobby?
—Why does God want us to obey our parents?

Illustrate the Story

If you have budding artists in your family, they may want to illustrate the story of Bobby. Use a long piece of paper divided into sections. Let each person draw a scene about Bobby.

"Obey Your Parents" Poster

Read the Bible words aloud. Help your children memorize them by saying them out loud together several times. Then let the children say them alone.

Next, give each child a magazine and let him find a picture that reminds him of the verse. Talk about the pictures. Talk about why God wants children to obey their parents. Let the children glue the pictures on a sheet of paper. Add the Bible words. Hang the pictures where they can remind the children that God wants them to obey their parents.

The Obey Game

Here is a game to help reinforce the concept of obedience. First are commands for your children to obey. These are followed by rewards. Let each child take a turn to obey and receive his reward.
1. Go to your room and bring back your favorite stuffed animal. Reward: A ride on Daddy's back.
2. Give Mommy a kiss. Reward: A trick from Mom.
3. Go wash your hands. Reward: Tickle Dad.
4. Find something in your room to pick up and put away. Reward: Play follow the leader. All family members must do what you do.

A Family Song

Let your children make up a song to the "Mulberry Bush" tune. Start with "This is the way I . . ." and end with "I will obey my parents (or mother or father)."

GRANDPARENTS' NIGHT

GOAL
To emphasize the importance of grandparents and to show love and appreciation for them

BIBLE WORDS
"Let us love one another, for love is from God" (1 John 4:7).

FAMILY ACTIVITIES
Here are a number of activities from which to choose for this special Family Night. Use the activities you feel your children will enjoy doing for or with their grandparents.

If the children's grandparents are unable to be with you, you have two options. You could have a night to talk about Grandpa and Grandma and make some things to send them. You could call them and let each child have a specified time to talk. You might also ask grandparents ahead of time to send a letter to the children, perhaps some pictures, and some kind of surprise or suggestion for an activity.

The second option is to adopt grandparents from the church or neighborhood. It is my feeling that all children need the influence of older people in their lives. If your children's grandparents are dead or live far away, adopting an older couple would be a great experience for both you and your children, as well as for the couple you adopt.

Grandparents Poster
You will need a large sheet of paper or poster board, scissors, glue, felt-tip pen, and magazines.

Everyone is to look for pictures that remind him of Grandpa or Grandma (for example, an older woman cooking, a man taking small children for a walk, a favorite food of a grandparent, and so forth). Let the person who chooses a picture tell you what caption to put beneath the picture. For instance, "I love Grandpa because he goes on walks with me."

At the top of the poster print "We love you, Grandpa and Grandma." Present this to Grandpa and Grandma at the end of the evening. Let the children explain the pictures.

A Picture for You
You may prefer to have your children draw a picture ahead of time to present to their grandparents.

Tell Me a Story
From the following list of words let each family member choose a word to give to Grandpa or Grandma. The grandparent must respond by telling a story from his or her childhood based on the word. Here are the words: barn, pet, afraid, trouble, fun, vacation, cry, church, school.

Telling on Grandpa and Grandma
Here's where you can get into the act. Think of a story from your childhood that involves something interesting about your parents. Have a good time "telling on" Grandpa and Grandma.

Talent Show
Let each child do a special talent for Grandpa and Grandma (sing a song, do a somersault, draw a picture, make a funny face, etc.).

Show and Tell
Each child may bring something from his room to show and tell to Grandpa and Grandma.

Timothy's Grandmother
The Bible tells us about a boy named Timothy. His mother's name was Eunice and his grandmother's name was Lois. They told Timothy Bible stories, such as Noah and the ark and Daniel in the lions' den.

Because of his mother and grandmother, Timothy learned to love God. When he grew up he became a missionary and told many people about Jesus and God (2 Timothy 1:5).

Read a Story
Let the children choose a Bible storybook for Grandpa and Grandma to read to them.

Grandparents' Favorite Dessert
Let the children serve their grandparents' favorite dessert.

End with a circle of prayer with each family member thanking God for Grandpa and Grandma.

DAD'S SPECIAL NIGHT

GOAL

To honor Dad as a special person and the leader of the family

BIBLE WORDS

"Honor your father and your mother" (Exodus 20:12).

FAMILY ACTIVITIES

Dad, tonight is your night. You are to be honored as the head of the family. This means you must be honorable. As Mom and the children prepare for this Family Night, perhaps you should take a few moments to examine your own life to see if you are the kind of person your wife and kids can look up to and respect. Be honest with yourself. Are you setting the kind of example they can follow that will lead them to follow Christ?

Honoring Dad

Mom, this night should be organized by you and the children. Prior to Family Night, get together with your children to plan what you will do. Make a "Dad Is Special" book. Use ten or more sheets of construction paper or typing paper. Punch holes and tie with ribbon. Have scissors, glue, and magazines and/or catalogs on hand. Help the children look for pictures that show things Dad does for and with his family, or that show things Dad particularly likes. Let the children cut and glue the pictures into the book. On the cover print "Dad Is Special."

Plan a special dessert to serve Dad on his night.

Let one or all the children present Dad with his book. Maybe you would even like to make a "gold" crown for Dad.

Explain to the children that God has made the father to be the leader of the family, and that God wants children to obey their fathers. Read Ephesians 6:1-4 from a modern translation.

NOTE: If there is no father at your house, perhaps you can have a grandfather, a favorite uncle, or a father-substitute for this night. If this is impossible, then use ideas from other Family Nights that were particularly successful and popular with your children.

A Loving Father

Mom, tell this brief story of Jacob and Joseph:

The Bible tells about a special father and son. Joseph, the son, helped take care of his father's sheep. Joseph was a good helper.

Jacob, Joseph's father, loved his son very much.

One day he said, "Joseph, I have a gift for you. Here is a new coat." It was a beautiful coat of many colors. Joseph liked his new coat. He was happy that his father loved him so much.

Another time, Jacob told his son, "Joseph, I want you to go and see how your brothers are. They are out taking care of the sheep."

Joseph did what his father asked him to do. He obeyed his father.

Discuss:

—What was the son's name?
—Who was the father?
—What special gift did Jacob give Joseph?
—Did Joseph obey his father?
—Why does God want us to obey our fathers?
—Why are fathers important?

I Will Obey

This is a game to illustrate obedience to Dad. Explain that Dad will ask each child to do something. It may be something funny or it may be a serious request. As the child prepares to do whatever Dad asks, he is to say, "I will obey," then do what he was told.

Prayer Circle

At the close of your Family Night have a circle of prayer thanking God for Dad and his leadership.

OUR MOM IS SPECIAL

GOAL
To remind children that mothers have a special place in God's plan for families and that their own mother is extra special

BIBLE WORDS
"Honor your father and your mother" (Exodus 20:12).

FAMILY ACTIVITIES
Mom, tonight you are in the spotlight. This Family Night is planned to help you feel extra special. Sometimes mothers need to be reminded of their important role, especially if they are bogged down with doing dishes, cooking, washing clothes, perhaps changing diapers, and so forth. Today's society has tended to make women feel inferior if they choose to stay home and take care of their homes and families. Never forget that yours is a high calling, a special place in God's plan. You are particularly needed by your preschoolers. These are important years. Do all you can for your children now, while they are young and impressionable!

Attention, Dad! This Family Night must be planned and carried out by you and the children.

We Love You, Mom
Ahead of time, get with your children and make a "We Love You, Mom" book. You will need typing paper or construction paper, scissors, glue, ribbon, and magazines or catalogs. On the cover print "We Love You, Mom." Help the children find pictures that show moms with their children, or women doing things that Mom does. After the pictures are glued, let the children suggest appropriate captions. Start each caption with "I love Mom because . . ." and then finish with the child's suggestion. You will need to help a young preschooler word this. Punch holes in the pages and tie with ribbon.

Decide on a dessert that Mother will enjoy and that you and the children can prepare.

Start your Family Night with a special presentation. If possible, purchase a small flower arrangement or a single silk rose. Have one of the children give Mom her gift and say, "This is your special night, Mom. We are going to honor you." Then you, or an older child, read Proverbs 31:1, 27-30 from a modern translation.

Next, show Mom the special book you have made for her. Let each child show his particular page and tell one reason he loves her. After she has looked at the book, each family member is to give Mom a kiss and say, "I love you."

Mother's Request Time
Now Mom gets to make some requests. She might ask one child for a hug, one to rub her back, one to get her a pillow, and so forth.

A Bible Mother
After Mother is comfortable, tell this story:

The Bible tells about a woman named Hannah who wanted to be a mother. She wanted a baby to love and care for. But Hannah had no children. She was very sad.

Hannah's husband told her, "I'm sorry you are sad. I wish you could be happy."

When Hannah went to the tabernacle-church to pray, she asked God to give her a baby boy. Then Hannah went home and waited. After many months Hannah had a baby boy. She knew God had heard her prayer! She named her baby Samuel.

Hannah was a happy mother. She took good care of baby Samuel. She loved him very much. And Hannah thanked God for her baby Samuel.

Discuss:
—Why was Hannah sad?
—What did she do at the tabernacle-church?
—Did God hear her prayer? How do you know?
—What do you suppose she did for baby Samuel?
—What does Mommy do for you?

Prayer
End your Family Night with each person thanking God for making Mother special.

Dessert
Have the table set with the good dishes and use candlelight. This will make Mom feel special! Serve her first and insist that everyone use his best manners. Don't forget the clean-up afterward!

FAMILIES FORGIVE EACH OTHER

GOAL

To help family members understand what forgiveness is and to know that they need to forgive each other

BIBLE WORDS

"Forgive, and ye [you] shall be forgiven" (Luke 6:37, KJV).

FAMILY ACTIVITIES

This concept is a difficult one for preschoolers. If you can find a book that explains forgiving in preschool terms, read this to your children. The book *Sorry* would be appropriate for older preschoolers and elementary-age children. If you do not have a book, give an example of forgiveness. It is always best to describe an abstract concept in concrete terms for preschoolers. For example, explain that forgiveness "is when" someone hurts you accidentally and says, "I'm sorry," and you say, "That's OK."

A Forgiving Father

Use this simplified version of the story of the prodigal son to show a father's forgiveness and love:

Jesus once told a story about a father who was very rich. One day the man's younger son asked for his share of the father's money. The son wanted to go to a big city and live the way he wanted to live. The father was sad to see his son leave, but he gave him the money.

After a while, the son's money was gone. He was hungry and had no place to live. He thought, "I was wrong to leave home. Now my money is gone and I have nothing. I wish I were home! I'll go back home and ask my father to forgive me."

And that's just what the son did. When he was almost home, he saw his father. His father was running to meet him. How happy his father was to see him! He put his arms around his son and hugged him.

The son said, "Father, I have been wrong. I'm sorry. Please forgive me. Just let me be a servant in your house. I'm not good enough to be your son."

But the father was so glad to have his son home.

He said, "Let's have a party and celebrate. My son who was gone is home at last!" And he forgave his son.

Discuss:
—How did the father feel when his son left?
—What happened when the son's money was gone?
—How did the father greet his son?
—What should we say when we have done something to someone?
—What do we say when someone says "I'm sorry"?

Role Play

This is a good story to role play. If possible, let the children dress in Bible-times clothes—a bathrobe and a towel or scarf over the head. The son should have something nice to wear when he leaves and take this off when he comes home. Let the children take turns being the father and the son.

Or, you may want to think up some everyday situations that will apply the concept of forgiveness. Let one child pretend to hurt another or break a toy, then tell the other child, "I'm sorry." Then encourage the hurt child to put his arms around the first child and say, "That's OK. I forgive you." Let the children take turns being each child.

Pray

Close with a prayer asking God to help each of you learn to forgive others.

Sing this song throughout Unit 7, whenever you need a break.

God Made My Family

WHAT MAKES A HAPPY FAMILY?

GOAL

To make family members realize that each person is needed to help make a happy family

BIBLE WORDS

"Be kind to one another, tenderhearted, forgiving each other" (Ephesians 4:32).

FAMILY ACTIVITIES

Again we have a concept that must be explained with concrete examples. Tonight, we will use five attributes that help make the family a happy one: love, kindness, cheerfulness, helpfulness, and forgiveness (a reinforcement of last week's concept). The main point is, however, that it takes everyone working together to make a happy family.

Love

If you have the book *What Is Love?* read this to your family. If not, find several pictures that depict acts of love. These might include someone hugging or kissing another, someone giving a gift, someone doing a favor, someone helping, and so forth. Make these into a little book and talk about each picture with the children. Then let them take turns telling what "love is . . ."

Kindness

Help each child think of a kind act he could perform for someone in the family right now. Then take time to do this. Make sure that the recipient says "Thank you" when the kindness is shown.

Cheerfulness

Tell this story:

Christie was a grouch. Her family called her the "Littlest Grouch"! She whined and complained all day long. She made everyone in her family feel very unhappy!

One day, Christie's mother and father decided the family ought to show Christie just what it would be like if everyone was a grouch like she was. So, everyone frowned and complained and whined and acted angry all day.

Christie felt terrible. It was a bad day. She thought, "What an unhappy family we have!"

Finally her mother explained, "Christie, we have been acting this way to make you see how you make us feel. When you are a grouch we are unhappy. We can't have a happy family unless everyone is cheerful and happy."

"From now on," said Christie, "I'm not going to be a grouch. I'll be cheerful. I want a happy family!"

Discuss:
—What was Christie's problem?
—How did her family help her?
—What did Christie decide to do?
—What happens in our family when someone is a grouch?
—How should we be? (cheerful)

Helpfulness

Get out the building blocks and have everyone work together to build something. Encourage each child to be helpful by handing someone a block or showing where to place a block, and so forth. Of course, a young preschooler will want to knock down whatever you build, so be prepared! Get him to help you build a tower when he knocks one down. Talk about how family members must help each other in order to have a happy family.

Forgiving

Just remind the children of last week's session on forgiveness and let them tell you what forgiveness is.

Picture a Happy Family

Give each person a piece of paper and crayons or felt-tip pens. Have everyone draw pictures of a happy family.

Dessert

Put all these elements together as you serve, eat, and clean up after dessert.

Pray together, asking God to help the family members work together to have a happy family.

A GIRL WHO LOVED HER BROTHER

GOAL
To help children realize that it is important to love their brothers and sisters

BIBLE WORDS
"The one who loves God should love his brother also" (1 John 4:21).

FAMILY ACTIVITIES

The Baby in a Basket

The Bible tells about a family who had a new baby boy. The baby had a mother and a father and a big sister named Miriam.

The family loved their baby very much. But they were sad. They lived in a land where the king wanted to get rid of the baby boys.

This family hid their baby boy for a while. But soon he was too big to hide. So the mother made a basket-boat that would float on the water. She lined the basket with soft blankets and put the sweet baby boy in the basket. Then she took the basket-boat to the river where the tall grass grew.

"Miriam," said her mother, "I want you to stay and see that nothing happens to your baby brother."

"I'll watch the baby, Mother," Miriam said.

While she was watching, a princess came to the river to bathe. The princess saw the basket-boat. She opened it and found the baby boy. She called him Moses.

Miriam ran to the princess. "Do you want me to bring someone to take care of the baby for you?" she asked.

"Yes," answered the princess.

Guess who Miriam got to care for the baby? That's right. Miriam ran and got her mother.

Moses' mother was happy her baby boy was safe. And Miriam was happy she could help care for her little brother.

Discuss:
—How did the mother hide the baby?
—Who was left to watch over the baby?
—Who found the baby?

—What did she call the baby?
—Who did Miriam get to care for the baby?
—Why was Miriam happy?
—How can you show love for your sister (brother)?

Make a Basket for Moses

Let each child make a basket and baby out of play dough. (*See page 69 for recipe.*)

Hide the Basket

After the baskets and babies have been made, let each child have a turn hiding his "Moses in the basket." Tell the child that he must stand where he can see the basket. The rest of the family must find the baby Moses.

Books

Spend some time reading storybooks to your children. *What Is Love?*, *Baby in a Basket*, and *My Baby Brother Needs Me* are all books preschoolers will understand and enjoy.

UNIT 8: A Love of Others

TELLING OTHERS ABOUT JESUS

GOAL
To make your children aware that they can and should tell others about Jesus

BIBLE WORDS
"Serve the Lord with gladness" (Psalm 100:2).

FAMILY ACTIVITIES
Because young preschoolers have no concept of distance, do not try to explain "foreign" missionary work to them. Rather, talk about what is familiar to them—their own area. Later, they will be introduced to work around the world.

If your children are kindergarten age and up, you may want to talk about missionaries, particularly those you are familiar with or that your church supports. They will also understand about giving money to missionary work.

Paul the Preacher
To get into the mood for tonight's story, make a tent. Put a large blanket over a table—a folding table or a larger one, depending upon the number in your family. Explain that this is a tent.

Paul was a maker of tents. But he did something else that was more important than that. He was a preacher, a helper for Jesus. He went everywhere telling people about Jesus. He told them that Jesus loved them. Many people were happy to know that.

Paul also had a young helper named Timothy who went with him. Once Paul and Timothy went to a riverside. There they met a woman named Lydia, and her friends. The women were singing and praying to God.

Paul and Timothy told Lydia and her friends about Jesus. They said, "Jesus loves you, Lydia."

Lydia and her friends were so happy to know that Jesus loved them. Perhaps Lydia said, "Thank you, Paul and Timothy, for telling me about Jesus."

Discuss:
—What did Paul do for a living?
—What else did he do?
—Who went with him to tell about Jesus?

—How did Lydia and her friends feel when they heard about Jesus?
—Do you think you could tell someone "Jesus loves you"?

Have a Song Fest
Start with "Jesus Loves Me" and then sing "Jesus Loves the Little Children of the World." Tell the children that many children have never heard about Jesus. Sing some favorite songs.

Paper Dolls
Help your children color and cut out the paper dolls on page 95. Talk about the children who live in other lands where they haven't heard about Jesus. Remind the older children that we can give money to help these boys and girls know about Jesus.

Books
Read the book *Who Is Your Neighbor?* to your older children. For young preschoolers, use the two books *God Loves Us* and *God Loves Everybody.* Talk about the people represented in the books who need to know that Jesus loves them. After you have looked at the books, use a toy telephone to call someone. Say, "Hello, _____. Jesus loves you!" Then let your little one try to say this.

GOOD FRIENDS NIGHT

GOAL

To talk about the importance of having good friends and being a good friend

BIBLE WORDS

"A friend loves at all times" (Proverbs 17:17).

FAMILY ACTIVITIES

Since this is Good Friends Night, invite some friends to share your evening. Invite someone with children near the ages of your children.

To start your evening, explain to everyone that this is Good Friends Night and you have invited guests because they are your good friends.

Two Bible Friends

Tell this story of two well-known Bible friends, David and Jonathan.

David was a poor shepherd boy. He worked hard taking care of his father's sheep. Jonathan was the king's son. He lived in the palace.

Jonathan and David became friends. They loved each other very much.

One day Jonathan said to his friend David,

"David, you are my friend. I want us always to be friends. Because I love you, I want to give you something."

Then Jonathan gave David his beautiful coat. "I want to give you something else," said Jonathan. And he gave David his bow for shooting arrows. He also gave him a belt and a sword.

David was happy. "Thank you, Jonathan," he said, "for these fine presents." David was happy Jonathan was his friend.

Jonathan was happy too. He was glad he could give his friend these presents. And he was glad they could be friends always.

Discuss:

—What did Jonathan do for his friend David?
—How did the two friends feel?
—Have you ever given something to a friend or done something nice for a friend?
—How did it make you feel?
—How else can we be good friends?

The "Good Friends" Game

Since good friends enjoy doing things together, each person must do something special with his friend (for example, sing a song, do a somersault, tell a story, etc.).

Table Games and Books

Provide simple games for the friends to play together. Little ones could also share books with friends. *Caring, Kindness, A Friend Is One Who Helps, What Is Love?* and *Buzzy Bee Storybook* are all suitable for tonight.

Dessert

Have a special dessert and let the children help serve their friends.

UNIT 8: A Love of Others

WE SHARE WITH OTHERS

GOAL
To help children learn what sharing is and know that Jesus wants them to share with others

BIBLE WORDS
"Whatever you want others to do for you, do so for them" (Matthew 7:12).

FAMILY ACTIVITIES
The concept of sharing is a difficult one for preschoolers to grasp because it is contrary to their nature. Preschoolers are naturally self-centered, so sharing is not easy to comprehend or to practice. But the concept of sharing should be introduced and worked on while the child is young. Gradually he will begin to understand and to go through sharing actions. He needs praise from you when he does share and encouragement when he has opportunities to share.

What Is Sharing?
For the benefit of your young children, make a sharing book. You will need to put this idea into concrete terms. On each page write a statement such as "Sharing is giving one of my cookies to _____ . . . . Sharing is letting _____ use part of my blocks. . . . Sharing is letting _____ look at my book with me." Add names of siblings or friends.

Think of as many examples of sharing as possible. Find pictures to illustrate these statements and help your child glue them in place.

Practice Sharing
If possible, let your children help you make cookies or some type of goodies to share with someone else. Perhaps you could have some of the preparation done ahead of time. Let the children participate as much as possible.

When the cookies are baked and decorated, take time to enjoy a few for dessert. Thank God for the cookies and for the opportunity to share.

Take the cookies to the person you have selected (perhaps a shut-in neighbor). While you are visiting tell the Bible story. You might also want to read a book or two, or have the friend read the book to your children. *Charlie's "Be Kind" Day* and *Sharing Makes Me Happy* would both be appropriate.

A Couple Who Shared
Elisha was a helper for God. He went many places telling others about God. Sometimes he had no place to stay at night.

A woman and her husband invited Elisha to a meal at their house. They shared their food with him. Elisha was glad they were willing to share.

The next time Elisha came to their town, he had a surprise. The kind couple had built a small room on the roof of their house for Elisha to use. The room had a bed, a table, a lamp, and a chair—everything Elisha would need. Elisha was happy. He was glad his friends wanted to share their house with him.

Discuss:
—What did the kind couple do first for Elisha?
—What surprise did they have for him later?
—How did Elisha feel about these kind things?
—Has anyone shared something with you?
—Have you ever shared something with someone?
—Can you think of a way you could share now?

ALTERNATE PLAN
If you decide not to make the cookies, here are some ideas for putting sharing into action.

Blocks
Play blocks with your children. Show them how they can share with each other. For a small child, sharing when he has several things is more realistic than expecting him to share his *only* teddy bear.

As you play, watch for opportunities. Say, "Thank you, Jeremy, for sharing your blocks with Brian. When we share we all have enough blocks to use."

Books and Crayons
Give each child a book and have him share with another person. Or, have the children share a box of crayons as they draw or color pictures.

Prayer
Close your evening with a prayer thanking God that you could have a happy evening of sharing.

BE KIND

GOAL

To help your children understand that God wants them to be kind to others

BIBLE WORDS

"Be kind to one another" (Ephesians 4:32).

FAMILY ACTIVITIES

Make sure everyone learns the Bible words. Have the Bible at hand so the little ones can take turns "reading" the words.

A Kind Woman

If possible, have a doll dressed in a dirty, torn garment to show when you mention the people who couldn't buy clothes. Then have a new garment to put on the doll in place of the old one.

The Bible tells about a kind woman named Dorcas. Dorcas' hands were busy every day sewing with a needle and thread. She was busy making clothes. And who were the clothes for? For herself? No, they were for other people—for grown-ups and for boys and girls. The clothes Dorcas made were for poor people who could not buy or make their own clothes.

How happy the people were when Dorcas made new clothes for them. Dorcas was kind.

Discuss:

—What was the kind woman's name?
—What did she do to show kindness?
—How did the people feel when Dorcas was kind to them?
—Can you do something kind for someone? What?

Kindness Search

Give everyone a magazine. Explain that each person is to find a picture of someone to whom a kindness could be done. Tell the children that kindness can be shown by a smile, a kind word, a touch, obeying, running an errand, and so forth (*you add to the list*).

When someone finds a picture he is to yell "I spy!" and then tell how he could be kind to that person or animal. If your children are too young to find their own pictures, cut out pictures ahead of time and lay them on the floor in the middle of your group. Let them pick up pictures and then ask them questions or give suggestions as to how they might be kind.

Books to Read

Charlie's "Be Kind" Day and *Kindness* are good books to read tonight. You could also use *God Loves Us* and *God Loves Everybody* with very young children. Simply point to one person at a time and talk about showing him kindness. "You can be kind to Grandpa by . . ."

A "Be Kind" Plaque

Have each child make a "Be Kind" plaque. On sheets of construction paper print the words "I will be kind to" and leave room for pictures to be glued below. Use faces cut from magazines or catalogs to represent a family member or friend (or actual faces from snapshots if you have some). Let everyone choose one or more faces to glue on his plaque. Add yarn hangers so the plaques can be hung up to remind the children of their promises. Talk about how the child can show kindness to the person he has chosen.

HELPING OTHERS

GOAL
To help your children see that Jesus wants us to help others—even those who may not like us

BIBLE WORDS
"We . . . are helpers" (2 Corinthians 1:24, KJV.)

FAMILY ACTIVITIES
If you have the book *A Friend Is One Who Helps*, use this to introduce tonight's Family Night. This book is based on the parable of the good Samaritan.

The Good Samaritan

Tell the story from Luke 10:30-37 in your own words, omitting details not relevant to preschoolers.

Role Play

Explain that you are going to role play this Bible story. Decide who will be the hurt man, who will be the good Samaritan (the good helper, for the benefit of very young preschoolers), the priest and Levite (or the two men who did not help). If you have access to some costuming, the children will enjoy wearing this.

Scene #1: A robber or two attack and rob the man. (*Make sure violence is kept to a minimum. Older preschoolers enjoy overacting.*) Robbers leave. Hurt man is lying on the floor.

Scene #2: One or two men walk by, looking but not stopping to help. (*If you are short of actors, have one man.*)

Scene #3: The good Samaritan (helper) comes along and stops to help the hurt man. Have this person carry a box of bandages, either packaged ones or just strips of old cloth) to put on the wounds. Then he helps the hurt man to the "inn." You may have Dad be the donkey if it will not cause the children to start giggling.

Scene #4: The good Samaritan pays the innkeeper to take care of the man.

You may need to shorten the play considerably so that you can do it over, allowing children to exchange parts. Everyone needs to be the hero at least once!

Discuss:
—Which man did what God wanted him to do?
—What does God want us to do when we see someone who needs help?
—Tell about a time when someone helped you.
—Tell about a time when you helped someone.
—Make a list of ways you could help your family or help others.

"Good Helper" Project

During the next week encourage each family member to become a good helper. When someone does something very helpful, he will be allowed to wear the "Good Helper" badge you will make tonight. Let the children help you make this out of construction paper (*cover with clear, self-adhesive plastic to make it last*).

Helping Chart

Make a "Helping Chart" to keep track of the helpful deeds the children do this week. At the side make a list of helping jobs they can do, leaving room to add new ones during the week. At the top list the days of the week. Help the children add their names when they help. Commend each child for whatever job he performs.

Just for Fun

Blow up a balloon. Explain that the balloon must be kept in the air at all times. You may use hands or heads to keep the balloon aloft.

Dessert

Let each child have a responsibility either in preparation, serving, or cleaning up after you eat. Make sure you thank each one for his help.

PEOPLE WHO HELP US

GOAL

To help family members appreciate policemen, firemen, and other community helpers

BIBLE WORDS

"God is good" (Psalm 73:1).

FAMILY ACTIVITIES

This Family Night would work well done in two evenings if you plan to make the visits suggested. You will need to call the police station and the fire station ahead of time to see if you can visit them and what time is most convenient.

Policemen Help Us

Look through magazines and newspapers with your children to find a good picture of a policeman. Let the children glue this to the front of a sheet of typing paper that has been folded in half.

Have a family discussion on what policemen do for us. List these things on the left inside page. On the right page write a thank-you note to the police department in your area.

Have each family member thank God for policemen who protect us.

Trip to the Police Station

Take your thank-you card to the police station. Give it to the person in charge. Ask if your children may look at one of the police cars, and maybe even sit in it and blow the siren. If possible, have someone give you a brief tour of the facilities.

Remind the children that "God is good" to us to give us good helpers like the policeman.

Build a Town

Use building blocks to build a town. Include houses, streets, and the police station. Use toy cars and let one of the children be the policeman. Have him watch for traffic violations, help someone across the street, and so forth, all positive ways policemen help us. You will want to let all the children have a turn being the policeman. It is important that you build in the minds of your children a good image for the police, because many young-

sters pick up bad concepts concerning lawmen.

Firemen Help Us

Make a thank-you card for firemen. Follow the same procedure for the policeman's card.

Have a time of prayer with each family member thanking God for firemen who help keep us safe.

Fire Drill

Make a simple plan for what your family should do in case of a fire. Then have a fire drill.

Mock Fire

Let your children pretend to be firemen putting out a fire. Stress the fireman's concern for human life, his bravery, and so forth. Tell the children that "God is good" to give us firemen to protect us.

Going to the Fire Station

Take the thank-you card and deliver it to the fire captain at the fire station. Ask if your children may tour the station. The captain may be willing to reinforce the importance of a fire escape plan, not playing with matches, and so forth. Children are more apt to listen to someone other than parents!

Helper Song

Make up some verses to the tune of "Mary Had a Little Lamb." Start with something like this: "The policeman is a friend of mine, friend of mine, friend of mine. The policeman is a friend of mine. He will keep me safe." "The fireman is a friend of mine . . . he puts out the fire." Add verses about other community helpers, if you want, such as "The doctor is a friend of mine . . . he will keep me well." Use the book *God Loves Everybody* as a visual as you sing.

Montage of Helpers

If you would like to include other community helpers, make a montage. You will need to look for pictures of the mailman, baby sitter, grocery clerk, nurse, dentist, librarian, and others. At the top print "Thank You, God, for helpers."

Dessert

Stop at a restaurant for dessert tonight. Remind the children that the waitress is a helper too.

CORRELATED ITEMS

The following items have been recommended in this book. They are on the preschool level and fit with the concepts of the book. Numbers after the items tell which units they are used. If you live near a Christian bookstore, take time to look at the items and purchase those your family will enjoy the most. You may also order from Standard Publishing. Items marked (*) are especially suitable for young preschoolers.

BOOKS

The Big Flood (#3639; $.98)—1
The Great Big Boat (#4917; $4.95)—1
Ark Full of Animals (#2707; $3.95)—1
How God Gives Us Series (*Peanut Butter*, #3626; *Apples*, #3627; *Ice Cream*, #3628; *Bread*, #3629; *Chocolate*, #3585; $.98 each)—1
What Is Faith? (#3643; $.98)—1
*God Loves Us (#2692; $.98)—1, 2, 8
*God's Animals (#2693; $.98)—1, 3
*God's World (#2695; $.98)—1, 6
What Is Love? (#3642; $.98)—1, 7, 8
Baby Jesus ABC Storybook (#3624; $.98)—2
The Very Special Night (#3637; $.98)—2
The Gift of Christmas (#4914; $4.95)—2
Christmas Is a Time for Singing (#3581; $.98)—2
*Baby Jesus (#2689; $.98)—2
Jesus, God's Son (#2705; $4.95)—2
Growing Up (#4911; $3.95)—2
Growing As Jesus Grew (#4924; $4.95)—2
When I'm Afraid (#4900; $4.95)—2
Courage (#4930; $4.95)—2
The Little Lost Lamb (#4919; $4.95)—2
Saying Thank You Makes Me Happy (#3623; $.98)—2
Buzzy Bee Says "Bee Happy" (#3625; $.98)—2, 4
Buzzy Bee Storybook (#3641; $.98)—2, 4, 8
*God Loves Everybody (#2691; $.98)—2, 8
House Full of Prayers (#2707; $4.95)—2, 5
*My Friend Jesus (#2699; $.98)—2, 4
God Made Puppies (#3635; $.98)—3
God Made Kittens (#3636; $.98)—3
Thank You, God, for Winter (#4905; also *Spring*, #4906; *Summer*, #4907; *Fall*, #4908; $4.50 each)—3
*My Bible Book (#2697; $.98)—3
The Very Best Book of All (#3591; $.98)—3
Bible Stories Make Me Happy (#3522; $.98)—3
Obedience (#4926; $4.95)—4
Honesty (#4925; $4.95)—4
A Child's Book of Manners (#3633; $.98)—4
Jesus Makes Me Happy (#3520; $.98)—4
*I Learn to Pray (# 2696; $.98)—5
*God's Colors (#2694; $.98)—6
Thank You, God, for Wonderful Things (#4921; $4.95)—6
God's Beautiful World (#3634; $.98)—6
God's World of Colors (#3640; $.98)—6
God Made Me (#3597; $.98)—6
I'm Glad to Be Me (#4903; $4.95)—6
Thank You, Lord, for Me (#4912; $3.95)—6
All About Hands (#3593; $.98)—6
Busy Feet (#3594; $.98)—6
Sorry (#4897; $4.95)—7
Baby in a Basket (#4918; $4.95)—7
My Baby Brother Needs Me (#4901; $4.95)—7
Who Is Your Neighbor? (#3644; $.98)—8
Caring (#4928; $4.95)—8
Kindness (#4929; $4.95)—8
A Friend Is One Who Helps (#4909; $3.95)—8
Charlie's "Be Kind" Day (#3595; $.98)—8
Sharing Makes Me Happy (#3589; $.98)—8

INLAY PUZZLES

*Gifts From God (#2681; $1.19)
*God Cares for Us (#2682; $1.19)
*We Are Helpers (#2683; $1.19)
*We Go to Church (#2684; $1.19)
*The Baby Jesus (#2515; $1.19)
*Noah's Animals (#2516; $1.19)
*God's World (#2517; $1.19)
*Jesus Loves Little Children (#2518; $1.19)
God Loved Us and Sent His Son (#2533; $1.19)
God Watches Over Baby Moses (#2534; $1.19)
Jesus Loves Me (#2535; $1.19)
Jesus Loves the Little Children (#2536; $1.19)

GAMES

Buzzy Bee's Garden Game (#2640; $5.95)
Bible Animal Dominoes (#2650; $4.95)
Noah's Ark Lotto (#2687; $4.95)
Happy Day Card Games (*Noah's Ark*, #2547; *Bible ABC's*, #2546; *Bible Match 'em*, #2632; $1.29 each)
Sewing Cards (*My Friend Jesus*, #2194; *Bible Animals*, #2193; *Birth of Jesus*, #2240; *God's Gifts*, #2241; $2.95 each)
Spinner Games (*Noah and the Animals*, #2551; *Where's Baby Jesus?* #2563; $1.39 each)
Bible Picture Pairs (*Bible ABC's*, #2662; *Bible Children*, #2663; *Bible Numbers*, #2664; *Birth of Jesus*, #2666; $2.50 each)

All prices subject to change without notice.

RECIPES AND PATTERNS

Finger Paint: Mix 1 cup of mild powdered soap or detergent with ⅓ cup liquid starch (or ¼ cup water). Beat with a rotary beater until mixture is like frosting. (Add more liquid or more soap if necessary. Starches and soaps vary.) Add a few drops of oil of wintergreen if desired. Add food coloring last.

Finger paint may also be made with wallpaper paste and water. Add food coloring or powdered tempera after mixture is desired consistency.

Play Dough: Mix 1 cup flour, ½ cup salt, and 2 tsp. cream of tartar in saucepan. (Do not omit cream of tartar.) Add 1 cup water, 1 tbs. cooking oil, several drops of oil of wintergreen if desired, and food coloring. Cook, stirring, for three minutes or until mixture pulls away from pan. Knead immediately. Store in airtight container. This recipe makes enough dough for about six people.

Harp pattern for story of David and King Saul.

Use with story of the lost sheep.

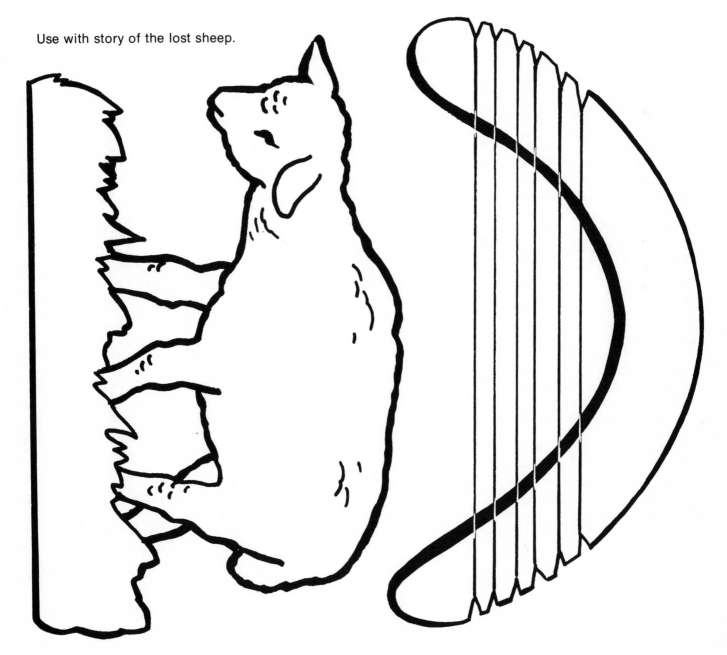

Jesus finger puppet

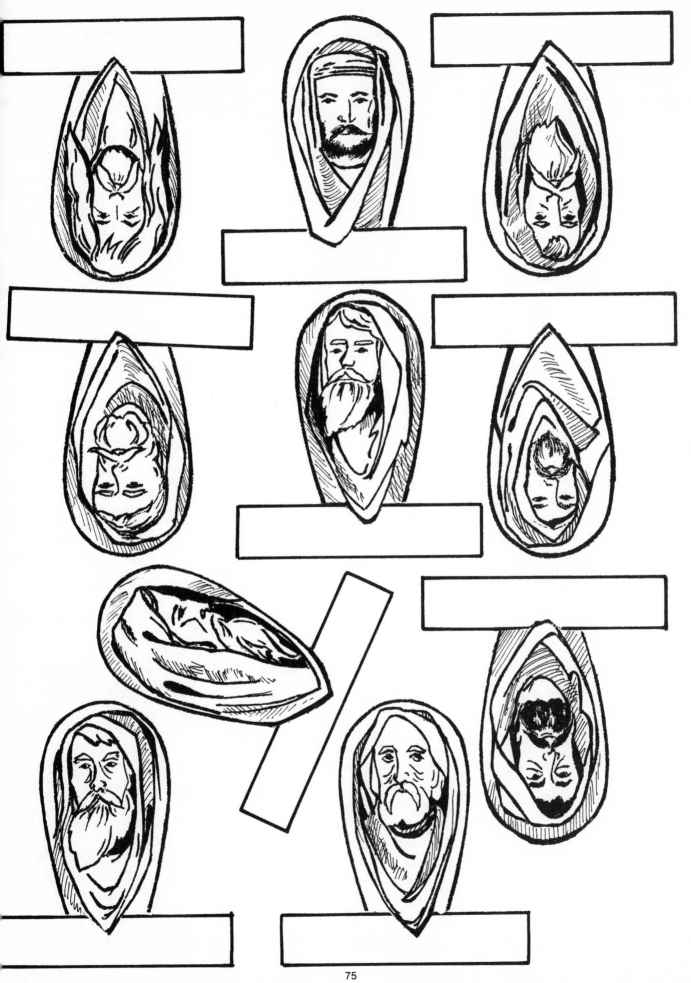

77

God made everything. Tell one thing God has made that you like.

You may ask a Bible question. The person who answers correctly may spin the bottle next.

God wants us to be happy. Laugh as loudly as you can.

Stand on your head.

Do a somersault.

Run to the kitchen and get a cookie for each member of the family.

The Bible is God's special Book. Tell your favorite Bible story.

God wants children to love their fathers. Give Daddy a kiss and hug and say, "I love you."

God wants children to love their mothers. Give Mommy a kiss and hug and say, "I love you."

Who had a coat of many colors? If you know the answer, spin again.

Think of an animal that Noah took on the ark. Make a noise like that animal. The person who guesses the animal can spin next.

The Bible says that friends are important. Who is your best friend?

Dad is to be your horse. Each child can ride him two times around the room.	Make a funny face.
Each family member must find a hat to wear the rest of the game.	Tickle Mom or Dad.
God made pets. Go get your pet and do a trick with him for the family.	Mommy must bark like a dog.
Jesus said we are to help others. Have you helped someone today? If so, spin again.	Who was Jesus' mother? If you know the answer, spin again.
What is your favorite color? Find something in the room that is your favorite color.	What baby was placed in a basket-boat? If you know the answer, spin again.
There is a special surprise for you. Ask your dad where it is and share it with the rest of the family.	Who built a big ark-boat? If you know the answer, spin again.

Who was the shepherd boy who played a harp? If you know the answer, spin again.	Jesus said, "Follow me." Play follow the leader. You are the leader. Family members must do what you do for the next three minutes.
Where was baby Jesus born? If you know the answer, spin again.	Pantomime a Bible story.
What men came to see baby Jesus and brought Him gifts? If you know the answer, spin again.	Go to your room and bring back the toy you like best. Show it to the family. Tell why you like it.
Who was put into a den of lions? If you know the answer, spin again.	Tell Mom something funny to do.
Give your brother and/or sister a big hug.	Tell Dad something funny to do.
Who is your favorite Bible man? Who is your favorite Bible woman?	Love is kind. Do something kind for the person closest to you.

Make a "joyful noise unto the Lord." Have a family rhythm band. Each family member must get a "musical" instrument (pots and pans, sticks, spoons, bottles, etc.).

Where was Jesus born? Spin again if you know the correct answer.

The whole family should wrestle on the floor for the next three minutes.

What kind of work did Jesus' earthly father do? Spin again if you know the answer.

Jesus loves you. Sing "Jesus Loves Me" for the whole family.

Do a puppet show.

Think of a Bible person. The rest of the family must guess who you are thinking of.

Draw a picture and send it to your grandpa and grandma. (You may save this activity until after the game.)

The Bible says "obey your parents." Mother can tell you something to do now and you must obey her.

Go to your room (all children). When Mom and Dad call, come back and find special surprises they have hidden.

Dad must take everyone out for an ice cream cone now (or everyone gets a serving of ice cream at home).

What was the name of Moses' sister? If you know the answer, spin again.